"A thoughtful and highly informative book. Joanne Travers reminds professionals that when families are supported, informed, and positively engaged in the habilitative process, there are simply no limits to what can be accomplished. In addition to practicing professionals, I believe that this book would be of great value to students who are preparing to work with the families of infants and children with hearing loss."

*Richard Seewald, Ph.D. / Distinguished Professor Emeritus, Western University, London, Ontario, Canada*

"The author has provided uncommon and practical insights for supporting parents and professional carers of children with hearing loss. Her perspectives on a variety of issues confronted in caring for children with hearing loss should enrich cross-cultural understanding of the unique but surmountable challenges of ensuring optimal quality of life for the affected children throughout the life course."

*Bolajoko Olusanya MD, PhD / Developmental Pediatrician, Lagos, Nigeria*

"An important aspect of this book focuses on the realities and needs of families coping with deaf children. It fills an existing gap in the bibliography intended for training of those in human resources, whose services are directed to the families of the Deaf. It should be a mandatory text of consultation for doctors, teachers, audiological staff, psychologists, counselors, speech therapists, and families, as it shows itself to be an excellent educational resource with a view to self-care, emotional healing, and empowerment of families with deaf children."

*Onelia Aybar, Director of Education / Instituto de Ayuda al Sordo Santa Rosa, Santo Domingo, Dominican Republic*

"Childhood hearing loss and deafness is one of the most common health conditions facing families in low-resource areas of the world, causing a disruption of the educational, economic and social fabric of the family and community. There is increasing recognition that the family and community play a critical role to provide optimal care and rehabilitation of these children. But the focus is all too often solely on the child, leaving caregivers to struggle. Joanne Travers has many years of experience empowering families of children with hearing loss and now offers her expertise to healthcare and educational providers. This book provides a wonderful guide to help families through this process."

*James Saunders, MD / Professor of Otology & Neurotology, Geisel Medical School at Dartmouth, Dartmouth Hitchcock Medical Center, New Hampshire, U.S.A.; Co-Chairperson, Coalition for Global Hearing Health; Medical Director, Mayflower Medical Outreach*

"This is a great book for parents, caregivers, and practitioners who want the best for the hearing-impaired child they love. This book shows how to support character strengths and well-being that can help children. With personal stories, evidence-based science, and practical tools, Joanne lays out a positive, hopeful, and optimistic path for parents and practitioners who support children with hearing loss."

*Megan McDonough / CEO and Founder, Wholebeing Institute; General Manager, RISE, Kripalu, Massachusetts, U.S.A.*

"I have known and have come to trust and depend on the practical wisdom of Joanne Travers. Ms. Travers has artfully crafted this instructional and insightful textbook. All those who care for children with hearing loss who read and heed the sound advice she offers in this text will be far better equipped to fight the good fight."

*Ron Brouillette, PhD / Education Specialist, Arizona, U.S.A. Former CEO of Global Deaf Connection and Deaf Education Consultant for WHO and CBR*

"This is a great resource for professionals and parents. The tools and exercises are particularly very well documented and are simple and easy to implement and use! I look forward to applying these strategies in my practice and with our parent support group."

*Vahishtai Daboo, LSL Cert. AVT / Co-founder and Managing Trustee, VConnect Foundation, Mumbai, India*

"The tools provided in this book are comprehensive and take on a holistic approach which will greatly enhance the practitioner's knowledge base. Joanne's personal experience as a parent of children with hearing loss makes *Coaching and Empowering Caregivers of Children with Hearing Loss* even more valuable, and her years of service and experience in countries like the Dominican Republic and India provide insight and consideration to cultural differences. Whether in-country or if traveling to do mission work overseas, this resource is outstanding and highly recommended!"

*Nicole Hunter-Diaz / Hospital Administrator, Centro Cristiano de Servicios Medicos, Los Alcarrizos, Dominican Republic*

"A very informative, practical, and holistic guide for caregivers and professionals who are involved in the habilitation process of hearing-impaired children. Joanne's personal experience in working with so many families has given this book valuable insights which would immensely assist parents and professionals. It is an inspirational resource with many practical tools and notably includes a strengths approach to help parents and professionals."

*Fatema Jagmag, Audiologist and Speech-Language Pathologist / Co-Founder, VConnect Foundation, Mumbai, India*

# Coaching and Empowering Caregivers of Children with Hearing Loss

## *an approach to foster well-being*

Joanne N. Travers

*A publication of Partners for A Greater Voice*

PGV

COPYRIGHT © 2019 by Joanne Nance Travers

ALL RIGHTS RESERVED. No part of this book may be reproduced in any form, stored in a retrieval system or transmitted, in any form or by means of electronic, mechanical, photocopying, or by other means without written permission from the author, except in the case of brief quotes embodied in articles and reviews.

*Coaching and Empowering Caregivers of Children with Hearing Loss*

*an approach to foster well-being*

Travers, Joanne, 2019

ISBN: 978-1-7338235-0-0

Library of Congress Cataloging-in-Publication

PCN: 2019938140

Includes bibliographical references

Issued in print and electronic formats

Cover design by JB Designs, Inc.

First Edition made possible by Hear the World Foundation, a division of Sonova

Printed and bound in the United States of America

Published by Partners for A Greater Voice, Inc.

www.greatervoice.com

This book is a reference work based on the author's educational and qualitative experience. The information contained herein is in no way to be considered a substitute for consultation with a duly licensed mental health professional.

# **DEDICATION**

This book belongs in the hands of all practitioners who work tirelessly, day in and day out, to combat hearing loss in their countries. Some of these practitioners are alone in their hearing health quest to help families with limited income and resources. We dedicate this book to them and to the tens of thousands of families and children they serve. We hope our parent approach to well-being weaves its way into their hearing health and habilitation practices.

# Contents

Note to the Reader .................................................................................................... 11
Essential Programs to Coach and Empower – a PGV training program ............... 12
Preface ...................................................................................................................... 15
Why This Resource Matters ..................................................................................... 19
How to Get Started .................................................................................................. 22
How to Approach this Book .................................................................................... 24
Introduction: About a Parent ................................................................................... 26
Why is Well-being Essential to Parenting? .............................................................. 28

## PART ONE:
### Positive Psychology Framework

Overview Positive Psychology ................................................................................. 33
Optimism and Positive Mindset .............................................................................. 35
Cultivating Gratitude ............................................................................................... 38
Growth Mindset ....................................................................................................... 39
Parent Emotions ....................................................................................................... 43
Parent Vision ............................................................................................................ 47
Parent Belief ............................................................................................................. 48
Meaning .................................................................................................................... 51
Stress is Not a Bad Thing ........................................................................................ 54
Resilience .................................................................................................................. 56
Coping with Hearing Loss ....................................................................................... 59
Four Coping Strategies:
    I. Mindfulness .................................................................................................... 61
    II. Meditation ..................................................................................................... 66
    III. Introspection ............................................................................................... 68
    IV. Self-Care ...................................................................................................... 70
Positive Change ........................................................................................................ 72
Learning and Development ..................................................................................... 74

Visualizing Goals ........................................................................................................................ 76
Summary ................................................................................................................................. 78

## PART TWO:
### Building Capacity: Personal Resources, Leadership, Character Strengths

Introduction ............................................................................................................................. 82
Parent Potential ...................................................................................................................... 83
Personal Resources ................................................................................................................ 86
Thoughts on Leadership ........................................................................................................ 90
Leadership and Trust .............................................................................................................. 93
Emotional Intelligence, a Leadership Asset ......................................................................... 94
Fostering Parent Leaders ....................................................................................................... 97
Character Strengths ................................................................................................................ 98
   *What are VIA Character Strengths?* ................................................................................ 99
VIA Institute's Classification of 6 Virtues and 24 associated Character Strengths ......... 100
How to Coach using Character Strengths .......................................................................... 102
   *Identifying and Spotting Strengths in Parents* ............................................................. 102
   *Exploring Character Strengths* ...................................................................................... 103
   *Applying Strengths* ......................................................................................................... 103
   *Applying Strengths in Difficult Situations* ................................................................... 105
   *Helping Caregivers Apply Strengths with their Children* .......................................... 105
Character Strengths Associations ........................................................................................ 108

## PART THREE:
### Parent Supports

Introduction ........................................................................................................................... 112
Parent Supports ..................................................................................................................... 113
Coaching and Empowering ................................................................................................. 117
Empathetic Listening ............................................................................................................ 119
Relationships ......................................................................................................................... 123
Encouraging Parent/Child Interaction ............................................................................... 126

Comments on Critical Thinking... 127
Coaching Parents on Communication Opportunities... 130
What Do Parents Want? A Parent Education Survey... 135
Parent Support Groups... 137
Case Study: V-Connect Foundation... 142
Reducing Barriers to Stigma of Hearing Loss... 144
Fostering Hearing Loss Awareness in Schools... 146
Comments on Community Collaboration... 148
Summary... 149

# PART FOUR:
SUPPLEMENT I:
   Comments on Disability... 155
   The Convention for Rights of Persons with Disabilities (CRPD)... 157
   The Focus on Families... 160

SUPPLEMENT II:
   Comments on Aural/Oral Communication... 161
   Expanding Hearing and Speech Services... 163
   Developing Listening Skills... 165
   Listening and Spoken Language Therapy... 166
   Comments on the Internet... 167

SUPPLEMENT III:
   How to Start a Parent Group... 168

# SOURCES AND RESOURCES:
ENDNOTES:... 173
BOOKS:... 179
WEBSITES:... 181

# ACKNOWLEDGEMENTS:... 183
# ABOUT THE AUTHOR:... 186

# LIST OF EXERCISES:

Reflect on Well-being………………………………………………………………………14

Exercise in Positive Visualization……………………………………………………37

Practicing Gratitude……………………………………………………………………….39

Adding Daily Affirmations………………………………………………………………42

Emotional Awareness……………………………………………………………………..46

Transforming Limiting Beliefs…………………………………………………………50

Assess Your Resilience……………………………………………………………………58

Mindful Breathing Exercise……………………………………………………………..65

Guided Meditation Practice……………………………………………………………..67

5% More Exercise……………………………………………………………………………71

Practice Self-Compassion………………………………………………………………..73

Reflect on Your Best-Self…………………………………………………………………84

Identify Your Personal and External Resources………………………………..89

What Styles of Management do You Relate to?………………………………..91

Emotional Intelligence Assessment………………………………………………….96

Exercise Your Character Strengths………………………………………………….110

Engaged Listening Assessment……………………………………………………….120

Questions for Reflection…………………………………………………………………122

Moments of Joy……………………………………………………………………………..125

"IF THEN"………………………………………………………………………………………128

Use of these exercises should be cited and referenced as, *Partners for A Greater Voice, Inc. Content derived from Essential Programs to Coach and Empower, Ipswich, Massachusetts, U.S.A. All rights reserved, 2019.* Exercises in this book are available for download at www.greatervoice.com.

# Note to the Reader

*Coaching and Empowering Caregivers of Children with Hearing Loss, an approach to foster well-being* is a resource and motivational guide for practitioners of audiology, education, counseling, aural/oral communication, social services, habilitation, and primarily intended for those who touch the lives of families of children with hearing loss in low- and middle-income countries. The book is a culmination of the author's experience with Partners for A Greater Voice (PGV), its mission work with parents, and mind/body health. It shares an approach to caregiver well-being that engages and empowers parental caregivers of children with hearing loss.

The words "parent" and "caregiver" are used interchangeably to describe a parental caregiver. PGV recognizes many caregivers as aunts, grandparents, and adolescents.

The World Health Organization states:

> A person who is not able to hear as well as someone with normal hearing – hearing thresholds of 25 dB or better in both ears – is said to have hearing loss. Hearing loss may be mild, moderate, severe, or profound. It can affect one ear or both ears and leads to difficulty in hearing conversational speech or loud sounds. The majority of people with disabling hearing loss live in low- and middle-income countries.[1]

The word "hearing loss" is used throughout this book. Around the world, different words and local dialect are used to describe children who do not hear and speak. Persons may be called "deaf," "hard of hearing," "hearing impaired," or "deafmute." Some communities label children with hearing loss by calling them "stupid" or simply "mute." These labels are not meant to be derogatory, yet sometimes inappropriate labels perpetuate and influence stigma. PGV supports practitioners and parents with the language they choose, and we encourage the use of "hearing loss" to dismantle any label.

This book is not a replacement for clinical and psychological supports caregivers may require. We recommend caregivers seek professional counseling with a certified and licensed mental health professional or therapist when necessary. Practitioners may choose to delve deeper into topics that extend beyond the scope of this book. For this purpose, a resource section includes websites and books on positive psychology.

Enjoy reading and learning from this resource. May it inspire a new direction of thought in the interventions provided to families of children with hearing loss where parent support and empowerment are needed and evolving in the world.

# ESSENTIAL PROGRAMS TO COACH AND EMPOWER — A PGV TRAINING PROGRAM

What drives empowerment? What motivates and enables parents to feel good about their involvement in their child's development? What balances the demands of family and routines with a child's communication, education, and health needs? How best can we coach parents through years of support the family may need? How can caregivers influence positive change in systems of hearing health and habilitation supports? Answers to these questions are based on the diagram shown below. Partners for A Greater Voice (PGV) has identified five domains as having a positive impact on caregiver welfare. The essential need to focus on caregiver psychological well-being is supported by all areas contained in the outer circles. Training interventions related to these five domains have a tremendous influence on caregiver achievement.

**The Partners for A Greater Voice Diagram on Caregiver Well-Being**

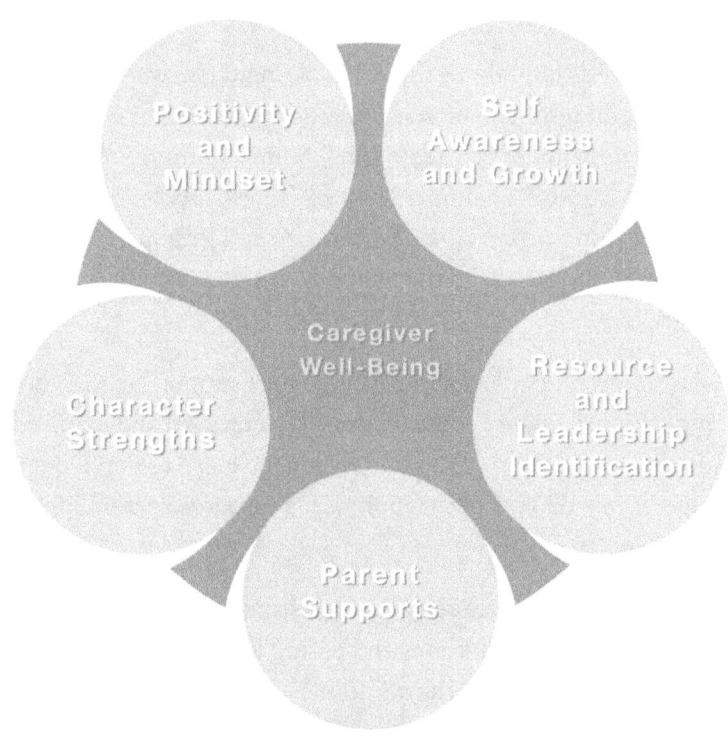

Partners for A Greater Voice's (PGV) Essential Programs to Coach and Empower is a convergence of theory and practice gathered from the field of positive psychology, hearing habilitation, and parent supports. It is an in-country training program that has emerged from the author's parenting experience, holistic practices, and international missions. Inspired by decades of international mission work, years studying positive psychology, and parenting children with hearing loss, the author confers that caregiver empowerment is crucial in the developing world where services for children are limited. The diagram on well-being, created by PGV, becomes the necessary tool to enable them.

**Objectives of Essential Programs to Coach and Empower include:**

- Promote positivity in caregivers
- Maximize ways to engage and enable parents
- Foster parent ability and potential
- Improve ways to communicate with caregivers
- Establish relational and resourceful supports
- Prepare caregivers emotionally for their journeys to raise children with hearing loss

*Coaching and Empowering Caregivers of Children with Hearing Loss, an approach to foster well-being* emerged from Essential Programs to Coach and Empower and supports a belief in the potential of every parent. It is an important resource that lays the foundation of parental well-being and enablement. Every culture cannot possibly be represented in one resource, but PGV believes the strategies and activities presented here are universal and can be applied in any community, regardless of socio-economic status. All parents, regardless of education and position in society, can develop with positivity, optimism, resilience, character, and autonomy. There are many opportunities to help parents thrive as leaders of their child's development when informational and social supports include ways to encourage positive thinking, learning, character strengths, leadership skills, and peer relationships. To improve outcomes for children in low- and limited-resource environments, it is critical that caregiver well-being is the goal and remains at the core.

The PGV organization supports family-based initiatives, clinics, academic institutions, and community-based programs interested in fostering the power every parent has for affecting child outcomes. Essential Programs to Coach and Empower is a hands-on interactive training program that is offered onsite. Practitioners are welcome to reach out to PGV for more information about in-country training and to explore the organization's website for further resources (www.greatervoice.com).

# REFLECTION ON WELL-BEING

Reflect on the Partners for A Greater Voice (PGV) diagram of well-being and review the following statements. Observe your mindset and the relationship you have with parental caregivers. How best can you engage parents in optimism, personal growth, confidence, strengths, positive relationships, and potential?

Parents who are optimistic are motivated to help their children succeed.

Outcomes for a child's success are improved significantly when parents are curious about and engaged in learning about hearing health care and communication development.

Parents who have healthy relationships with their family members and their practitioners are more trusting, confident, and inspired to respond to their children's needs.

When parents connect with other parents, they often engage in personal narratives; stories about life at home or at school enhance perceptions of their abilities to parent a child with hearing loss.

When parents become aware of and acknowledge their abilities and other competencies, they feel inspired and engage with their children and others with more confidence.

As caregivers become aware of the nature of their emotions triggered by hearing loss and stigma, they engage in and nurture their children's learning and communication with compassion and intention.

Positive and nurturing practitioner/parent relationships that embrace parent views and beliefs and encourage parents to respond to their children's needs and development with more determination.

# PREFACE

I have always held an unwavering attitude to maintain a positive mindset since the day my daughter was diagnosed with progressive, severe hearing loss in 1994; she was one year old. My son was diagnosed with moderate to severe hearing loss 23 months later shortly after his birth. The vision my husband and I embraced for our children was an auditory-verbal philosophy, mainstream inclusion, and a future full of education and employment opportunities. Learning to listen and speak would become the foundation for their success. As their parents, we needed to prepare them for their independent lives. Retinitis pigmentosa (progressive vision loss), diagnosed years later, (caused by a recessive gene called Usher's syndrome), as well as my daughter's attention deficit disorder and learning disabilities would not get in the way of her living a full and complete life.

In the mid-1990s my world revolved around my daughter and son who were diagnosed as babies with hearing losses. I sacrificed my dreams to provide for my children and delved into a world of hearing assistive technologies and auditory verbal therapy. Most friendships I cultivated back then were with parents of children with hearing loss who sought mainstream school placement and an aural/oral education. Each parent had a story to tell, a perspective I was to gain, and a problem I was to explore and learn from. Bountiful narratives emerged as I worked through my own grief, worry, and fears. Their beliefs, emotional journeys, successes, and advocacy were a vast playground for my education and ways to raise my own children. This amazing group of families gave me deep insight into the accomplishments of children and parenting achievements that equipped me and helped my own children prepare for independent and successful futures.

From the first day of our children's diagnosis until their college graduations, my husband and I built our lives around their social, emotional, physical, and cognitive needs. We made many sacrifices to ensure their well-being and success. They would thrive in school and life and become self-advocates. They would build resilience and strive for what their hearts dreamed and desired. They would make their own decisions and choose lives and jobs which would bring them happiness. They had every right to learn, to make their own decisions, and to become viable participants in society.

In those early years of my children's lives, I unconsciously allowed stress and grief to seep under my skin. Those emotions drove me to learn and excel in gaining necessary supports that would carry me through years of persistence and curiosity. I found courage to pitch myself at everyone I could learn from, and I creatively applied my abilities and talents every day in support of my children's needs. My love of learning led me to embrace oral deaf education and to seek essential parent supports that would carry my journey from Massachusetts, U.S.A. to nearly every continent of the world. In small ways, I shared the knowledge I gained and the theory that all children, no matter their economic status and culture, could thrive like any hearing child when given supports. I placed my children's well-being above my own.

My journey in hearing health and auditory-verbal therapy began when I started a parent network in my home state of Massachusetts in the United States. In 1995, gathering a group of supportive families who coped with hearing loss and children's mainstream education was seldom done successfully. Most parent networks failed to sustain themselves. They were griping sessions or groups of parents who viewed their children as dis-abled. I wanted a group that was optimistic, hopeful, and filled with opportunity for families and their children. With a strategic plan in place, practitioners of aural/oral education for the deaf would embrace this calling. Together we established a group that remains active to this day.

That group, called Parent Connection, grew to a network of over 170 families. This accomplishment was remarkable back then when emailing or cellular texting was not available. By today's standards, parent groups reach into the thousands on social media, but in the mid-1990s the phone was our only connection. Meetings and newsletters catered to the interests of members, and monthly programs were founded on the premise of empowering and engaging parents in their children's mainstream, aural/oral education. The national and state disability laws were on our side and we could advocate for their needs with success. Because parent-to-parent connections need to be cultivated through personal communication, face-to-face meetings and interpersonal relationships had to be developed. Groups of parents met regularly, nearly every month. Family gatherings brought entire families together for picnics and other fun events. Newsletters kept everyone informed. Children made friends. Parents made personal connections. In many ways our approach back then resembles the methodology needed in low- and limited- resource communities.

Parent Connection was not the only initiative I was interested in pursuing. I had graduated with a master's degree in International Management in 1993 (one year before my daughter was born), and I was motivated to put my education into practice. My passion and perseverance guided my heart and desire to support not only my own children but the needs of parents and practitioners in developing countries, with an interest to serve those in resource poor communities. While coordinating events and activities for Parent Connection, and working for a college, I incorporated Parents for A Greater Voice. After one year of planning and research, I left my job as an International Coordinator of grant funded, economic development initiatives, and I delved into the global need to support practitioners and parents in low- and limited- resource communities. A board of five directors encouraged and supported me. I found myself boarding a plane to the Dominican Republic alone, with no Spanish skills. My knowledge of French would only take me so far on this Caribbean island.

Advocating for the advancement of aural/oral communication and parent empowerment, our programs led to starting parent groups, establishing a school for the deaf, constructing two speech-language therapy rooms, collaborating with several schools for the deaf and audiology clinics, donating audiology equipment, and coordinating hundreds of training and education workshops for teachers and parents. Our missions invited dozens of experienced practitioners from the United States. They volunteered to help inform, demonstrate, and train other practitioners proving how children with hearing loss can learn to listen and talk. We translated hundreds of pages of educational materials into Spanish because there was limited auditory-verbal content in Spanish at the time. Information in this field did not travel quickly back then. We carried hundreds of hearing aids and our training manuals, bound with plastic spirals, and filled our suitcases with books, therapy toys, and other donated essentials.

My international and parent group endeavors, plus part-time employment and the care of my family, impacted my health. Layers of physical and emotional stress began to show in my body after years of devotion to the hearing and learning needs of my children, other families, and international service projects. I found myself trying to cure plantar fasciitis, lower back pain, carpal tunnel, neck stiffness, knee injuries, and an imbalance of the digestive system. Passion sees no boundaries when there is an opportunity to help others and be involved in this important work to educate and inspire. My love of learning, perseverance, and curiosity carried me forward, and I pushed my body through years of physical pain and exhaustion. I inevitably came to realize the importance of self-care.

Physical and mental stress manifest in the body differently; not all parents experience these same physical maladies, but as a witness to stress and anxiety in parenting experiences I learned how caregiver well-being must take precedence. I became introspective, practiced yoga and meditation, and created psychological space to see my role as a supportive parent and caregiver more clearly. It took me nearly three years to unwind and release the physical and emotional exhaustion that had accumulated over a decade.

Through it all, I was resilient in the presence of the darkness and loneliness I sometimes felt. I saw hope in any challenge that I faced. Optimism and love help balance worry and grief, and my children depended on me as a model of hope, perseverance, and moral character. Their social and emotional well-being was paramount, even when their mother put her own health on hold to support their needs.

It takes courage to face one's emotional grief and find peace. Reality can help the mind and heart see a purpose more clearly. Fostering my well-being would renew my spirit and help me deepen PGV's programs and support to families. I needed to home in on a focus for the organization, rather than serve across the wide spectrum of information in hearing health and habilitation.

In 2014, the board of directors evaluated PGV's 35 international projects, donations, and training initiatives to determine the organization's priorities. The common thread among all programs was our parent education and empowerment. The success of the parenting journey meant well-being needed to become a priority. Rather than focus on the outcomes of children, why not focus on the outcomes of parents who influence the success of their children? I enrolled in Wholebeing Institute's positive psychology program and became certified in 2015. Two years of continued study, conference presentations to practitioners, and pilot work in the Dominican Republic and India solidified PGV's approach to parent empowerment and engagement. Psychological well-being was essential, and it became the necessary foundation to effective parent empowerment in all PGV training initiatives. Living a healthier, happier journey is an inside job.

In over twenty years of parent education and dozens of international service missions, PGV has sought a holistic approach to help parents thrive in their journey and become empowered. Regardless of social status, education level, culture, and economic discord, primary caregivers have innate abilities and strengths that enable them to be successful in the care they give to their children. PGV's Essential Programs to Coach and Empower emerged throughout 2015. Their new approach to foster caregiver well-being equips low- and limited- resource communities with new tools and perspective in family centered care.

PGV believes using a positive psychology approach enhances coaching practices that can effectively reduce stigma and improve the way caregivers respond to hearing loss and engage with their families, children, and communities. Positive psychology gives attention to what works, rather than what impedes. To affect positive change, practitioners can influence caregivers' journeys by fostering their psychological well-being.

Throughout this book, PGV's business model on well-being and interventions describe ways practitioners find new inroads to the parent heart and mindset. A goal of this resource is to foster parent's learning and self-knowledge. Further, it provides tools to influence parent's self-esteem and responsiveness to their children and hearing health practices. In focusing on parent self-efficacy, potential, and essential parent supports, PGV's domains of well-being become the platform for parent empowerment and engagement in their children's success.

# Why This Resource Matters

Hearing health and habilitation practices throughout the world are complex in that they include a spectrum of audiological and educational services that address diverse populations with varying hearing conditions and habilitative needs. The number of persons affected with hearing loss is currently estimated to be around 466 million, and the majority reside in low resource countries, according to The World Health Organization (2018). Approximately 34 million children are affected by some degree of hearing loss globally (and recent analysis suggests this number is inconclusive and may very well be underestimated in low resource environments). The World Health Organization also states that more than 60% of childhood hearing loss could be prevented.[2] And hearing loss might not be the only disabling condition. Learning challenges, attentional deficits, and other physical disabilities may be present.

Parenting a child with hearing loss in low- and limited- resource countries is undoubtedly challenging. Parents have limited income and struggle to find social, emotional, and informational supports that can help their children communicate and learn. Social stigma, insufficient access to Hearing Assistive Technologies, inaccessible education services, inadequate healthcare, and potentially no family services are other factors. In many low- and limited- resource communities, children with hearing loss are unable to communicate at levels comparable to hearing peers and experience significant delays in communication, speech, and socio-emotional growth. Communication is especially important and necessary for children with complex needs.

Because hearing loss carries considerable stigma in the developing world, it has always been Partners for A Greater Voice's mission to instill positive supports to caregivers who struggle with their children's delayed communication, limited resources, and education. Far too many parents live alone with their emotional and physical grief, and sadness and loneliness emanate in the eyes among parents every place we travel. Parents feeling good about themselves and exploring their innate potential can lead to improved responsiveness to learn, develop skills, and acquire personal supports.

The support and counseling caregivers receive must therefore include consideration of their psychological well-being. According to many developmental psychologists, caregivers have the most influence on children's social, emotional, physical and cognitive development when they have good self-perception, emotional health, economic stability, and skills to nurture children successfully.

To address the hearing, communication, and learning needs of children, practitioners collaborate with the parents to inform and empower them. It is the job of every practitioner to educate and support the family, yet practitioners might be the only professional parents encounter. Practitioners must find essential time to coach and engage caregivers not only as partners in their children's development, but as independent leaders who are mentally prepared for their journeys. Ultimately, practitioners must balance the learning and communication needs of children with the emotional needs of parents and important lessons that engage parents in hearing health and habilitation.

However, practititioners who work with families of children with hearing loss also struggle to empower and enable parents as partners in their children's development. Challenging social and economic conditions often deter caregivers from fully engaging in order to promote their children's progress and development. The complexity of the global hearing health industry and parenting children with hearing loss in low- and limited- resource countries must therefore include strategies to more effectively foster caregivers' well-being. And practitioners who work with families must be equipped with training and interventions supportive of caregiver mental health and essential to igniting potential and building parental capacity.

For this reason, PGV shares their training approach and domains supportive of caregiver well-being that may not be currently applied in hearing health and habilitative practices. All exercises included in this book have been developed and offered by PGV to practitioners and parents in many communities. While the domains to foster well-being apply across all demographics and sectors of society, practitioners can explore them in different situations and choose interventions that are appropriate for parents and their cultural environment. Though there is no guarantee that all caregivers will pursue a strategy to become self-aware, optimistic, and engaged in happier journeys, practitioners can decide which interventions in this resource will best support their caregiver's mental health and learning journey.

Parents need guidance, and they listen to those with experience, knowledge, and wisdom. Audiologists, psychologists, rehabilitation coordinators, teachers of the deaf, and other specialists are powerful allies for parents who cope with their children's hearing loss and their role as caregivers. With appropriate support and coaching focused on positive psychology, practitioners serve as a source of inspiration to parents as they learn and grow.

Although positive psychology is emerging throughout the world in nearly every sector of human services and business, it is not widespread in hearing health practices. However, recent policy and disability groups address caregiver capacity and responsiveness in positive ways. There are a host of programs globally that address caregivers' skills and ways to inform, educate, and empower them. A positive psychology approach may be needed to boost their effectiveness.

The positive psychology framework presented in *Coaching and Empowering Caregivers of Children with Hearing Loss* distinguishes itself from other resources with the goal to influence positive mindsets and well-being of caregivers. Engagement and empowerment find their roots in knowledge, yet parent effort and motivation come from within. The ability to draw upon intuition, beliefs, and abilities becomes essential for caregivers. Parents can identify talents and strengths in different ways. Coaching helps them discover qualities that, when put into practice, can enable positive, healthy, and independent behavior. In the journey to raise competent and happy children with hearing loss, parents must unearth their potential. In their willingness to engage in personal development, parents become the nurturing caregivers they are capable of being. And when empowered parents respond to the hearing, language, and education needs of their children, they drive progress in hearing health services for all children with hearing loss.

What is needed are safe and secure environments for parents to learn and grow as capable caregivers motivated to participate in their children's development in productive ways. There is a global interest to scale up early childhood development, parent responsiveness to nurturing care given to children, and inclusion for children with disabilities. This movement involves early identification initiatives as well as increased access to professional training, education programs, and parental capacity building. These undertakings align well with an essential need to advance psychological supports given to parents.

Though online webinars and training programs are more available today than ever before, many locations in the world have poor connectivity to the internet or have little money to invest in training. There remains an overwhelming urgency to support practitioners who serve families, but there are just not enough accessible training programs offered to support coaching and engaging caregivers in many countries. To PGV's knowledge, no publication directly addresses the psychological well-being of caregivers of children with hearing loss in low- and limited- resource communities and involves all the domains of well-being presented in this book.

PGV hopes this resource fills the gap and broadens awareness of the psycho-social supports needed by caregivers of children with hearing loss so that they can successfully engage in their journeys to raise their children. PGV believes that now is the time to scale up caregiver well-being as important and critical to child development and outcomes in developing countries.

# How to Get Started

## STEP ONE:

*Settle into a chair or comfortable place to look through the book at leisure; read the Contents and become familiar with the layout of the book.* There is an Introduction, four Parts, Supplements, and Resources. Each main part has several elements: Concepts, Exercises, A Note for Practitioner, additional information in text boxes. Scan through the book to get familiar with the format and information. You may wish to begin by reading the Introduction entirely and leaving other parts for another time.

## STEP TWO:

*Keep an open mind.* As you read each section or part, remember to embrace all content. This book summarizes many different subject areas. Some content may be new or unfamiliar to you. There is so much available information that it is impossible to include it all in one resource. For this reason, we offer "Resources and References" at the back of the book should you wish to delve deeper into content.

## STEP THREE:

*Choose one part that interests you most and find a quiet space to read it.* Set aside time to read this part and try to read the whole section! While each part is somewhat autonomous, reading the entire book is important because it provides a global picture and view of parent interventionism and coaching practices.

## STEP FOUR:

*Commit to reading all sections within a period of time.* Think of completing the book within one month, or a reasonable amount of time that you can manage.

## STEP FIVE:

*Reflect on and practice interventions before* using them with parents. In other words, you can experiment and witness the personal effects and benefits of each exercise before coaching caregivers. There is nothing more fulfilling than personal experience and the integration of knowledge that leads you down a path of assurance and success.

## STEP SIX:

*Take time to reflect on content and choose interventions that best apply to the parents with whom you work.* The intention is for you to apply interventions that work within the context of your practice and family services. Interventions may need to be individualized and sequenced in ways that best support the parents' learning and psychological needs. Throwing all the interventions at every parent is not practical, nor productive. Taking one intervention and using it with every parent may also prove ineffective. Every parent learns and works through supports differently, and practitioners must get to know their clients and their situation before deciding which interventions to apply.

# How to Approach This Book

*Coaching and Empowering Caregivers of Children with Hearing Loss* supports practitioners in the counseling and services they provide to parents who are learning to cope with their children's hearing health and habilitation, inclusion, and social stigma. Practitioners must find ways to support parents' sense of personal competence and positive belief in themselves as well as their children's ability to thrive, regardless of hearing loss and economic hardship. Supporting child success begins with developing **parent capacity** and encouraging a parent's innate potential.

Parents can become leaders of their children's development. They can learn to successfully raise their children in mainstream society. Children learn in different ways; they may approach learning auditorily, visually, or kinesthetically. In consideration of these learning styles, parents will develop skills to manage, nurture, and care for the needs of their children's hearing, communication, and learning when coached and supported effectively.

The information in *Coaching and Empowering Caregivers of Children with Hearing Loss* offers distinct interventions to inspire and guide caregivers in their journeys, break stigma, and limiting beliefs. Positive interventions and encouraging supports enable caregivers on many levels: support children's learning and communication, engage parents in their learning, build parent potential. Fostering positive psychological growth and parent supports are a foundation for caregiver responsiveness.

In addition to an introduction, appendix, and resources, there are four parts to this book with many sub-sections. Each part includes the following topics:

    I. Positive Psychology Framework

    II. Building Capacity through Personal Resources, Character Strengths, and Leadership

    III. Coaching and Supporting Caregivers

    IV. Supplements: Comments on Disability, Convention for Rights of Persons with Disabilities, Aural/Oral Communication, How to Start a Parent Support Group, Hierarchy of Listening Skills

*Coaching and Empowering Caregivers of Children with Hearing Loss* is a non-linear resource. Each part is a separate module containing short, succinct topics. Practitioners have busy schedules and they can read parts or segments at their own pace. Though subject matter may interrelate, practitioners can filter through the book in search of key topics and strategies that apply to their culture and situation. What may apply to one practitioner may not apply to another. In other words, practitioners can find what resonates with their interest and comfort level, and then integrate it into parent centered practices and programs at their school, clinic, hospital, or community center. All practitioners have different exposure to training in their area of expertise, and this resource is designed to enhance knowledge; it does not serve as a substitute for formal training.

Above all, PGV wants to foster caregiver well-being and encourage a conversation about ways to engage and enable parents in any community. The intention is to equip practitioners with new strategies and distinct interventions that build parental capacity and more effectively empower the caregivers they serve. Life can be challenging in low- and limited- resource countries, and it is even more difficult for a parent who must care for a child with hearing loss. With appropriate and sustainable support and coaching, parents can respond adeptly to the process of hearing health and habilitation with purpose and emotional preparedness.

Practitioners are welcome to study and explore concepts in this book more deeply before applying them in their practice. Further materials can be found in the list of resources at the back of this book. The organization welcomes a conversation about the subject matter and is available to plan on-site training designed to meet program interests and parent support.[3]

> **Parental Capacity** is the ability to parent in a 'good enough' manner long term (Conley, 2003). According to many practitioners, 'good enough' parenting means meeting the child's health and developmental needs, putting the child's needs first, providing consistent and routine care, and acknowledging problems and engaging with support services.
>
> *NSPCC Information Service, 2014.*

# INTRODUCTION

## ABOUT A PARENT, AN ORAL PRESENTATION

*I imagine she tries to put her grief aside, and wonders if her child is truly deaf. She senses it though; deep down she knows it and wants to help her baby. Most days she worries about her child's inability to talk, and she is unable to communicate like she does with her other children. She might make herself forget about it at times, pushing away feelings and pretending there is nothing wrong.*

*One morning, she wakes up with a plan to help her child. There is a doctor who travels from afar and tests hearing. Rumor has it that this group of people can fix a child's hearing. There are hearing aids they give for free, and maybe this can help her daughter communicate. She worries if her child will qualify for one. She feels nervous and scared about traveling the distance, but she goes anyway.*

*Her other children might stay with a family member, or she will bring them with her. There might be no one in the neighborhood to take them in. She is not going to work today, and she won't earn any money. She might not call her employer. She just won't show up to work.*

*No one says anything to her as she begins her journey to the doctor who will test her child's hearing. She passes neighbors and other people in her community. She feels their eyes upon her, and they silently glance down at her child and then back at her. She wonders if they know. They know. She walks steadfastly along the dirt path, firmly gripping her child's hand and feeling like a stranger in her community; warmth and moisture builds between their palms. The smell of burning trash, the sounds of people frying plantains and eggs seem foreign to her. She is not hungry today. She goes quietly about her business, taking the long journey by bus, on motorcycle, or by foot. She ignores the sweat that dribbles down her neck and back as the sun rises into the sky. There are no clouds today.*

*I sense her isolation and can almost feel the touch and warmth of the child near her. Thoughts churn inside her mind, as she keeps her child close. She journeys onward with anticipation. No one knows what to do with a child who doesn't hear or speak. In fact, she feels alone most of the time.*

*There is no one she can talk with about hearing loss, at least right now. Her heart is smothered with grief so strong that it upsets her belly, and she tries to forget about the sickness she feels and pushes through it. Maybe nothing can be done. Worry seeps into her skin.*

*People confront her about why she is a mother of a child who is mute and stupid and different. Words people express are often condescending and hurtful; they blame her. "You are the one that caused this child to be cursed," they say. It is hard to make sense of the slander. She grabs hold of a belief that this doctor will change all that.*

*The hours pass by in deep thought as she makes her way to the mission site. She grasps for hope and thinks there's a solution, a cure! This is her child's first hearing test, and she says to herself, "Everyone tells me nothing can be done to my child, but I'm going to try." Try again for the love she has for her child. Still, she has a purpose; God tells her this when she prays. Maybe it is her mind reminding her of her courage. Her strength of love and perseverance bubble up from her heart.*

*As she gets closer to her destination, she wonders if she will have to wait all day in the heat, hungry and exhausted among strangers. And when she finds a place to rest her aching feet, I envision her glancing around at dozens and dozens of other people waiting too. Some are old, some are young. Most look sad and tired too. Mothers cradle babies in their cloth slings. Toddlers huddle against their mother's side, scared of these new people and unfamiliar surroundings. She pulls her child closer.*

*There's going to be a hearing test today, and feelings of relief rise up from her belly to her engaged and discerning eyes. She tries to relax and tilts her head left and right to release a stiff neck. I see her wonder, "Is there truly a cure? Is there someone that will help me understand why? Is there someone that will talk to me about what I should do? Are there others here, like me, who feel the same?"* [4]

# WHY IS WELL-BEING ESSENTIAL TO PARENTING?

Parents make effective and positive changes in their lives as caregivers of their children when they feel good about themselves and when their actions facilitate good outcomes in parenting and child development. PGV sees positivity and psychological well-being as essential. To guide caregivers as empowered and enabled leaders of their child's development and to improve hearing health, well-being must become the central focus. Parenting a child with hearing loss and encouraging their responsiveness begins with what works best for parents.

Strengths awareness, positive relationships, leadership and parenting skills, and personal growth are all ways to successfully engage parents in the hearing health needs of their children. Capability and potential can carry parents toward the vision and goals they seek for their children, yet they need to be aware of their own mindsets and emotional challenges. This begins with an examination of parent hearts and minds. Parents engage more deeply when they are emotionally prepared to raise children with hearing loss. They may also be determined to support their children's needs and development when they embrace an optimistic view of their capabilities as well as their children's future. Receiving appropriate advice and counseling is equally as important as finding peace with life's parental struggles and ways to cope with hearing loss. Practitioners who want to empower caregivers of children with hearing loss should explore caregiver well-being and what parents think, believe, and feel.

There are several related perspectives and theories on psychological well-being. Dr. Carol Ryff's theory of well-being includes six factors: contentment, positive relationships, competency, autonomy, meaning or purpose in life, and personal growth. Incorporating these factors into the lives of parents who have children with disabilities, and whose journeys are that much more challenging than with children without impairments, becomes important. Ryff's study of well-being shows that the challenges faced in life must be balanced with rewarding experiences. Confronting reality, no matter how difficult,

---

**Psychological Well-being** is a theory developed by Dr. Carol Ryff and is achieved by a balance of both challenging and rewarding life events. Dr. Ryff defines six factors which contribute to an individual's psychological well-being:

1. contentment and happiness,
2. positive relationships with others,
3. personal mastery,
4. autonomy,
5. a feeling of purpose and meaning in life,
6. personal growth and development.

*Ryff's Scales of Psychological Well-being (2005); C.D. Ryff, "Happiness is Everything, or is it?" (1989).*

remains important. Predictors of psychological well-being also include optimism, resilience, acceptance, and a growth mindset.[5]

According to positive psychology experts, happiness involves three primary features: positive emotion, engagement, meaning. Dr. Martin Seligman developed a theory on happiness and well-being that suggests active involvement in *positivity*, *engagement*, and *meaning*, as well as positive *relationships* and *accomplishments*. In 2011, he describes these five factors using the acronym PERMA. Incorporating PERMA into anyone's life creates opportunity for positive change.

The PERMA model created by Dr. Martin Seligman suggests five core elements that help people reach a life of fulfillment, happiness, and meaning. It can be applied to institutions to develop programs and to help people. It further considers one's character strength and the application of human virtues; these underlie the PERMA model and lead to human flourishing (discussed in Part Two).

> **P**ositive emotions: self-esteem, optimism;
>
> **E**ngagement: vital involvement, being in *flow,* using character strengths;
>
> **R**elationships: meaningful connections;
>
> **M**eaning in Life: purpose and cultivating resilience;
>
> **A**ccomplishment: self-determination (Martin Seligman, Flourish, 2011).[6]

Further, Positive Psychologist Tal Ben-Shahar lists several strategies to well-being that include the following: giving yourself permission to experience the full gamut of human emotion (accept sadness, anxiety, envy, happiness, fear), engaging in physical exercise (three times per week), cultivating appreciation and gratitude, doing less (simplifying your life). He also states how science indicates how spending quality time with friends and family is the number one predictor of happiness and well-being.[7]

There are many ways to approach well-being in life. Closely related theories and practices on well-being become important to coaching and empowering caregivers of children with hearing loss.

**A NOTE TO PRACTITIONER:**

Partners for A Greater Voice (PGV) frames their coaching and empowerment approach around the factors and theories of well-being as well as the needs of parents coping with their children's hearing loss. The five essential domains shown in the PGV diagram below are necessary for successful parenting journeys to help children with hearing loss and are essential to caregiver well-being.

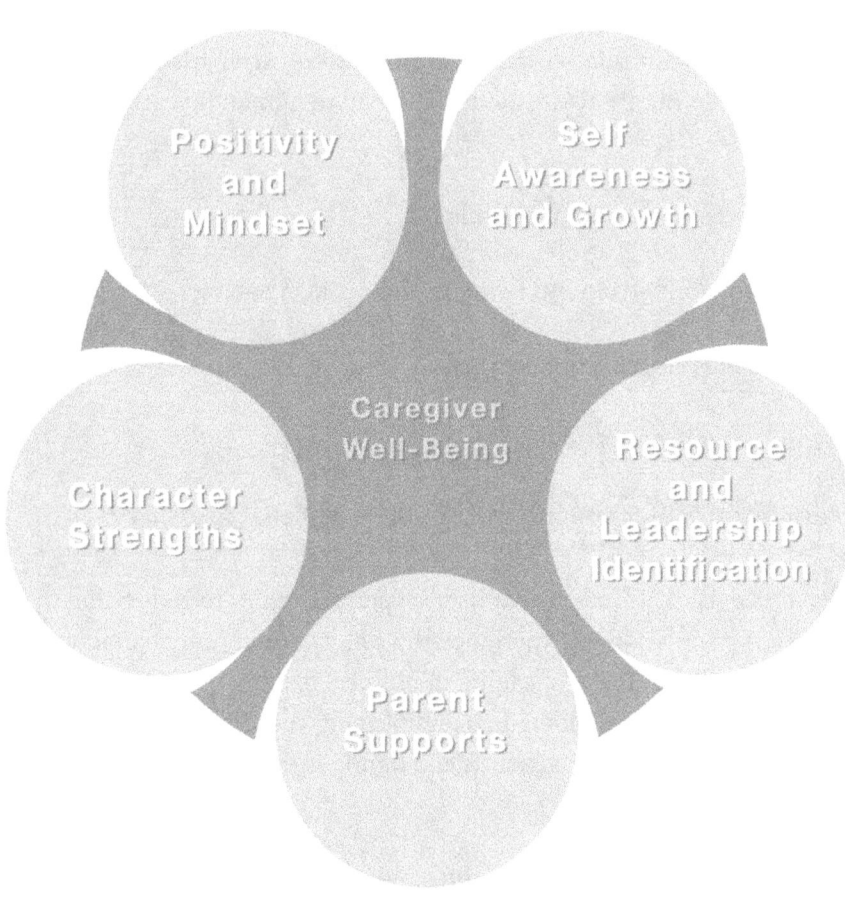

# Part One

# Positive Psychology Framework:
## Positivity, Mindset, Growth, Self-Awareness

# **OVERVIEW POSITIVE PSYCHOLOGY**

*"No pessimist ever discovered the secret of the stars or sailed to an uncharted land or opened a new doorway for the human spirit."* ~ Helen Keller

Positive psychology is the science of human flourishing, embracing many studies in the human condition and offering a new lens into the human spirit. It has emerged as an understanding of past satisfaction, present-moment experiences, joy, and well-being that leads to improved quality of life and human potential. Thriving in life includes the way we face challenges and respond to struggles. Rather than focusing on fixing or alleviating a problem, Dr. Martin Seligman, contemporary founder of positive psychology, examines the role of psychosocial factors and self-compassion in the enhancement of well-being and in support of personal growth and development.[8] Some major topics of interest in positive psychology include the following:

- Happiness
- Optimism and helplessness
- Mindfulness
- Flow*
- Purpose

- Character strengths and virtues
- Growth mindset
- Resilience
- Positive Relationships
- Self-Awareness

The field of positive psychology continues to offer insight and evidence of human flourishing.[9] Thousands of books, articles, and online references have been published in the field. Book stores and online book marts are bursting with self-help books that explain how optimism can lead to success. There are books on brain research and the power of positive thinking, goal setting, and gratitude. Countless other texts and online resources suggest holistic approaches to self-care, encouraging mindfulness, yoga and meditation practices, personal betterment, and financial success. All these resources have merit, especially in times of struggle or doubt.

Positive psychology is not all about being happy all the time. It is not about just showing a smile. Rather, it is a process to actively engage in strategies that promote well-being. Many factors of happiness suggest active participation in self-care, positive relationships, purpose, positive mindset, and personal growth. These aspects of well-being create opportunity for positive change and can lead to greater happiness. Further, the mental health of the parent often predicts how they interact with their children and this reflects children's outcomes.

A positive psychology approach can foster parent self-efficacy and determination. A happier and confident caregiver might engage in their life more meaningfully and perhaps try to improve a difficult situation. Parents who choose to better themselves and their feelings about hearing loss and their children's futures will grow confident. Parents who sulk in their guilt or disbelief of their children's hearing loss and future need nurturing supports to engage them in positive mindsets about their parenting journeys. Supports offered to parents lead them to feelings of empowerment. The process cannot be forced or rushed. Individuals take their own time to process and experience what is good for the mind, body, and soul. Self-care and knowledge acquisition are both rewarding and inspiring experiences.

On many levels, the application of positive psychology can help parents, especially those having difficulty coping with their children's hearing loss. Parents need to be mentally ready to engage. To become actively involved in their children's development parents need encouragement, inner strength, and a sense of purpose to see their children succeed in life. They need to understand their role as primary caregiver and partner in the hearing health and habilitation journey.

Practitioners can help children, but they cannot fully support every child's needs alone. Coaching caregivers therefore means supporting the parents in ways that make them feel good about themselves as capable and worthy participants. While caregiver mental health is a critical goal, applying effective strategies must support the parents' positive mind states as well as their willingness to take action.

> *"Flow" is a concept describing people's productive involvement in activities and their routines. It refers to being immersed in, focused on, and happily engaged in their present experiences. Author and psychology professor Mihaly Csikszentmihalyi states, "The best moments in our lives are not the passive, receptive, relaxing times… The best moments usually occur if a person's body or mind is stretched to its limits in a voluntary effort to accomplish something difficult and worthwhile."

# OPTIMISM AND POSITIVE MINDSET

"Optimism is faith that leads to achievement. Nothing can be done without hope and confidence." ~ Helen Keller

The optimist sees the glass half full and does not dwell on the emptiness of the glass. In the face of failure, struggle, or set back, optimists take steps forward to find solutions regardless of the difficult path. According to many studies on optimism, human flourishing requires the cultivation of positivity. In other words, optimism can be groomed. The potential to harness greater personal growth and positive development is often grounded on the mind's relationship with positivity. Martin Seligman claims 60% of people are somewhat optimistic. Other psychologists (Segerstrom, 2006) suggest upwards of 80% of people are optimistic. Regardless, there is an understanding in the field of psychology that challenging paths in an imperfect life can become glorious opportunities for development. It takes effort to persevere through difficult situations that can lead toward optimism and hope. We all need optimism to see us through the hard times.

The term "realistic optimists" combines both the positive outlook of optimists with the clear-eyed perspective of pessimists.[10] Realistic optimists use their realism to perform better, and they are not bogged down by unhappiness or negative thinking. Realistic Optimists are able to accept the truth and the reality of their circumstances. They believe change happens by working toward a goal or purpose. Thinking positively about an outcome or envisioning achievement are not enough; active, purposeful steps are necessary.

Optimism is a cognitive process and hope is emotion based. Optimism is a belief that we have an ability to handle adversity that inevitably may arise in the future.[11] Optimism is needed to help parents bounce back from difficult situations. A vision of the child's success in mainstream education and communication is an example of optimism. With feelings of hope, parents can remain positive in the face of adversity encountered at school or in social settings. Some parents persevere with hope through some of the most difficult situations. Hope guides them to resolve a problem or reach a goal.

When parents develop confidence, they say "yes" to opportunity. When they believe in their abilities, they achieve things. With hope and optimism driving them forward, a parent's **self-efficacy** emerges. Research indicates that parents are motivated to engage with their children when "the primary incentive for parents to become involved appears to be a belief that their actions will improve their children's learning and well-being."[12]

Albert Bandura, a modern psychologist, began studying human learning, eventually leading him to introduce *social cognitive therapy*. He views optimism as necessary for motivation and achievement. In order to achieve success, every person needs to believe he can succeed (self-efficacy). Realistic optimists plan well, access resources, stay focused, evaluate options, and execute well. Parents in low resource communities walk difficult paths and experience limited services and supports. They must find ways to believe in themselves and to feel confidence in the decisions they make for their children. When they are self-assured, they may engage in taking purposeful steps that support outcomes and goals they visualize for their children. Their progress often leads to feelings of gratitude, happiness, and fulfillment.

> **Self-Efficacy**
>
> Psychologist Albert Bandura has defined self-efficacy as one's belief in one's ability to succeed in specific situations. One's self-efficacy can play a major role in how one approaches goals, tasks, and challenges. It can determine whether an individual will be able to exhibit coping behavior and how long effort will be sustained in the face of obstacles.

Parents often need to understand what is possible for their children first; they need to envision a path and a future that leads to their children's success. Without knowing what is possible, how can parents see their children's potential? When parents are embraced by the optimism of others, they may feel inspired and see the possibilities for their children's future rather than fear it. Behavior is linked to perceptions, thus positive social interactions and optimism influence how people act.

Life with a disability is hard, particularly in developing countries where stigma and discrimination impinge on psychological well-being. Embracing hope, being in a positive relationship, and having good perceptions of the child's disability influence a parent's well-being.[13] Because high parental stress can be associated with frequent social and emotional problems of children, positive supports that help parents feel good about themselves and their children's future are vital.[14]

The parenting journey ebbs and flows with both challenges and successes, and parents benefit from developing a positive mindset with realistic expectations. Social supports become invaluable to parents because shared, realistic scenarios describe good and bad outcomes of children in social and academic settings. These positive and negative events help balance perspective. Thus, parents can engage in their children's development with specific intentions that they learn from the successful experiences of other parents and children.

Of course, more than optimism and success of other families are needed to enable parents of children with hearing loss. Other necessities include an ability to challenge limiting beliefs, to be aware of personal strengths, and to identify personal resources that carry parents forward in meaningful ways. The willingness to engage in personal growth, learning, and the emotional journey also strengthens how caregivers cope with stress and hardships.

**NOTE TO PRACTITIONER:**

Practitioners must consider ways caregivers harness a positive outlook. They must consider caregiver emotions and family supports that can instill realistic optimism. Gently reminding parents to imagine a glass half full with positivity may help. Practitioners can ask parents to shift the mind away from negative thoughts to positive ones. The child's first steps, the child's smile, the child's help with chores, or the child's first complete sentence are successes that can balance the challenges parents experience. Practitioners can express stories and examples of how parents and children overcome difficult situations and succeed.

Some parents are so filled with worry and fear that they have a hard time acknowledging how the mind can be persuasively negative. Brains are wired to learn, and though experiences differ, brains focus on survival and protection.[15] Balancing the fight or flight nervous system of the brain's response requires practice to identify thoughts that negate behavior and hinder progress, and then come to accept them. It takes practice to sort through thoughts and emotions that may be engrained in the neural circuits of the brain, and then to be optimistic and forward thinking.

When parents are unable to visualize a positive experience, coach parents to accept whatever feelings arise and have them reflect on the reality of the situation. It can be uplifting when parents identify and accept feelings that arise. When they release emotional tension, it allows psychological space to see things more clearly.

Seeing the positive in any situation builds awareness to know the difference; it is a practice of seeing the glass full of possibility. Refer to exercise below.

## EXERCISE IN POSITIVE VISUALIZATION

### Imagine the glass is half full rather than half empty.

Think of a challenging situation and describe it to the best of your ability: learning to read, teaching a child to speak, traveling long distances for services, experiencing the first day on the job. Visualize a glass, and then fill half of it with optimistic, honorable, and successful experiences of that situation. The empty part of the glass can hold the difficulties of that situation. How can you concentrate on the positive aspects of the situation, the glass half full, rather than the challenges and empty part?

# **CULTIVATING GRATITUDE:** *a strategy for developing positivity*

Gratitude is a state of pleasantness and linked with positive emotions.[16] When you are thankful or feel appreciation and kindness, there is something that triggers satisfaction. When you say a prayer of thanks or bless others in your life, goodness enters the heart. Appreciation and positive comments from people also instill greater feelings of worthiness and happiness. Research on gratitude links it to feelings of admiration, respect, trust, and positive regard (Storm & Storm, 1987). Gratitude is known to enable creative thinking, foster flexibility in thought, and broaden the ability to reason.[17]

Appreciation can be expressed in audible words, written in journals, texted on cellular phones, or written in letters of appreciation to someone. Writing in a gratitude journal can also evoke levels of well-being and feeling good about oneself. Research indicates being grateful promotes social bonds, positive emotional connections, and feelings of love.[18] Verbally expressing gratitude can shift the mind toward happier moments and satisfaction. Does this mean that gratitude exercises are the cure for unhappiness or a solution to grief? No, but being grateful can bolster morale and feelings of happiness.

Though gratitude studies are not specifically linked to parenting children with hearing loss, being grateful can help parents see the glass half full and instill a pleasing and positive outlook. For example, when parents focus on what they enjoy and appreciate even in times their children behave poorly or become difficult to manage, they see "the good in the bad" and "the glass half full" of gratefulness.

Gratitude is a powerful tool, and helps to buffer against threats, fosters resilience, and leads to improved problem solving (Creswell, 2013). According to research completed by Barbara Frederickson, the benefits of gratitude can also plateau. In other words, becoming used to something good can cause positive emotions to level out rather than stand out. Parents should understand that there is nothing worse than faking it. Gratitude must come from a place of sincerity and authenticity.

Practice gratitude daily. Use the exercise on the next page to help you get stared.

> ## PRACTICING GRATITUDE
>
> Help parents practice gratitude by working through the following steps.
>
> Think of your child and what you are grateful for: take five minutes in silence to think about different situations and not just physical attributes of your child.
>
> 1. Create a long list of things you are grateful for.
> 2. Look at the whole list and circle the top three things that are most important.
> 3. How do these moments support a positive outlook for you and/or your child?
> 4. As you move through your week, think of these grateful moments and remind yourself of this positive point of view.
> 5. Become aware of new moments, events, and interactions with your child that you genuinely are grateful for. Write them down or express them to a loved one.

## Growth Mindset

"Psychological struggles with difficult events can include negative psychological effects, but they may paradoxically also include highly meaningful outcomes."[19] ~ Pam Schmidt

Carol Dweck, a leading psychologist and researcher, coined the term "growth mindset" and "fixed mindset." She views growth-mindset as a powerful tool for motivation. A person with a growth mindset is someone who is willing to face challenges, make mistakes, and learn from those mistakes.[20] Those with a growth mindset keep on learning and expanding their perspective. Fixed mindsets, on the other hand, are based on limiting beliefs about a person's learning and intelligence. To appreciate a growth mindset, let's begin with the challenge parents face within themselves and with their children's hearing loss that create a fixed mindset.

One example of a fixed mindset is when parents' limiting beliefs do not consider children with hearing loss as capable human beings equal to other siblings or hearing children in the community. Parents may interact with people who have such limiting beliefs. Often an uneducated community makes comments that impose such restrictions on children's potential. Examples of limiting beliefs are expressed in these ways: "My child is not good enough." "My child will never be accepted." "Deaf people won't ever be able to talk." "My child will always be a deficit to this family." "I can't help my child." Such words betray a mindset that sees no opportunity for a child's potential and are fixed on a problem or challenge. A fixed mindset can lead to rumination of the problem rather than a solution or possible change. Getting parents to change their mindset requires a bit of neural rewiring of the brain. A grow mindset suggests that change is possible.

Optimism can cultivate such rewiring to support a growth mindset. Cultivating a positive, forward thinking mentality is a powerful practice. Sharing positive experiences of children and hearing loss can help parents see the possibilities of children's success in school, at work, or in marriage. Inspirational stories can shift perception. Parents need help visualizing the possibilities; they need to hear, feel, and experience things that help them break through stigmatized beliefs and thoughts that prevent them from forward thinking and engaging in the vision they have for their children.

> Forward thinkers, optimists, and problem solvers of the world often find solutions in difficult situations. Hope drives positive change, and conflicts are overcome by taking actionable confident steps (*Davis et al. 1998; Janoff-Bulman and Frantz 1997*).

When parents believe in the possibilities for their children, the mind refocuses. Thinking in itself does not necessarily lead to positive engagement, but those with a growth mindset will be open-minded to changing their attitudes and beliefs. Having a positive outlook matters and likely helps people engage more with things they care about.

A study on personal growth and a parent's emotional response to a child's developmental disability has found that stress release is linked to **benefit finding** experiences.[21] This "benefit finding" refers to "positive psychological change that is experienced from adversity and other challenges and helps people rise to a higher level of functioning"[22] (Encyclopedia of Positive Psychology, 2009). Forward thinkers, optimists, and problem solvers of the world often find solutions in difficult situations. When parents become aware of stress and their response to it, they may persevere or use forward thinking mentality to push through it. It has been found that mothers who are forward thinking cope well with stress. Their positivity becomes a foundation for coping and adjusting to their children's hearing loss, referred to as stress-related personal growth (Davis et al., 1998).[23]

We know from research that resilient people have growth mindsets. People living in low resource communities are often especially resilient because their hardships and challenges shape the way they think and behave. These parents have learned to be forward thinking in many ways. They care for their families, including ways to put food on the table, find work, find clean water, or keep their children from catching a cold.

Parents of children with hearing loss may have a growth mindset with respect to caring for a family's basic needs and survival, but they may have a fixed mindset around a child's deafness. Parents with growth mindsets think that change is possible. Cultivating a growth mindset around hearing loss is challenging, especially when no school or therapist are available to support the child's needs, or when discrimination and perceived disability hinder parents' ability to remain positive. It can also be challenging to encourage a growth mindset when children's language and learning is significantly delayed as compared to siblings and hearing children.

Metaphors about positive mindset and forward-thinking mentality are useful to shift parents' minds away from negative perceptions of their children or their children's hearing loss. In other words, in what ways are parents forward thinking around survival and care for family? Can this mindset shift toward the needs of their children? Consider these questions:

- *How has the effort of survival helped the parents succeed?* Can the parents transfer a mentality of basic needs to the child's hearing health?
- *What innovations have helped parents to find work and put food on the table?* Can the parents transfer some of their creative energies to caring for a hearing device or to helping children learn about their hearing loss?
- *What transpires when parents barter services (cooking, mending) or share resources (food, clothing) with others?* Can parents relate these interactions to ways they can build alliances with practitioners and other parents or to opportunities to explain the importance of communication and inclusion of their children?

It is not uncommon when caregivers of children with hearing loss are filled with negative events and thoughts which pervade the mind. Events that threaten self-integrity arouse stress and self-protective defenses that can hamper performance and growth.[24] Our fight or flight response system is designed to defend against harm to self and to protect self-integrity (integrity is the inner sense of "wholeness" deriving from qualities such as honesty and consistency of character). This fear-based response to life's challenges is natural in all human beings. Feeling socially connected, safe, and self-reliant reduces cortisol hormones that are produced when stress occurs.

What is needed is self-compassion and tender ways parents engage with love and nurturing care. Parent-child interaction can be a starting ground for shifting the mind to think about innate qualities parents have, such as love, kindness, and hope. Recognizing and working to limit negative influences means finding inner strength of character and self-compassion. Affirmations can help parents remain positive and can also promote forward thinking mentality. Research points to the fact that affirmations support coping and well-being. With regular practice, affirmations instill positive feelings and forward-thinking behavior. Dr. Barbara Frederickson, a researcher of positive emotions and a psychologist, states how the experience and practice of affirmations can boost positivity. Negative events are still valued, however. Her research suggests a good ratio of three positive thoughts to one negative thought. Negative events are important to balance the power of positive thinking.[25]

> Events that threaten self-integrity arouse stress and self-protective defenses that can hamper performance and growth. An intervention known as self-affirmation can curb these negative outcomes.
>
> *The Annual Review of Psychology, 2014*

### A Note to Practitioner:

When parents use affirmations consistently, they can learn to persevere through negative events and foster growth mindedness. Parents can take baby steps and practice one affirmation a week. It helps to notice how affirmations make parents feel or think. Positive change occurs when parents are willing to embrace good feelings and positive attributes about their life and circumstances. With daily practice, parents may report feelings of happiness and gratitude. Refer to the Daily Affirmations exercise below.

---

## ADDING DAILY AFFIRMATIONS

Consciously choosing a growth mindset and being forward thinking takes practice. People can choose comfortable ways to infuse positivity into their lives. Affirmations, a term primarily used in the practice of positive thinking and self-empowerment, is one way to encourage this behavior. Recent research suggests the use of affirmations can improve relationships, foster positivity, and induce self-esteem. Affirmations are solemn declarations similar to prayer, mantras, and chanting. Adding affirmations daily can be personally rewarding and constructive.

Examples of **affirmations**:

"May I be happy when I am with my child."

"May I remain calm and supportive with my child."

"May I use positive language near and with my child."

"May I smile with loving kindness at my child."

# Parent Emotions

*"The only way to change someone's mind is to connect with them from the heart."*
~ Rasheed Ogunlaru

In developing countries, practitioners are confronted with many challenges, including parent emotions and grief. Parents are scared, worried, fearful, or reticent of social stigma. They have little money or resources to support hearing health and the specialized education needs of their children. Parents are challenged in finding appropriate school placement. Harsh stigma and disability are major barriers to inclusion, in a school and a community. In all of this, parent hearts and minds are filled with grief and emotions about their children's hearing loss, but they often have a hard time identifying emotions. Grief is often viewed as stress, or they may not understand the degree of depression they experience. Sadness is often a feeling of loneliness. When parents understand the normalcy of the emotions they experience, they grow. Being aware of the cyclical nature of feelings helps.

Nearly all parents PGV has worked with in developing countries express worry, shame, guilt, loneliness, and depression. Shame and guilt are common, and this can lead parents to be reluctant to include their children in family or community events. Parents may worry or fear their children's future. They may feel unqualified or insecure about their ability to care for and nurture their children's learning. On top of responsibilities at work and home, parents may feel overwhelmed with the attention they must give to their children with hearing loss.

Parents in low- and limited- resource communities are often unaware of their emotions or how their emotions trigger behavior, whether positive or negative. Grief can lead to prayer, and prayer can lead to hope. Stress can either activate parent responsiveness to the needs of their children or it can lead to depression and inertia that leads to negativity, limiting beliefs, and feelings of incompetence. Many parents unconsciously push through stress because of their positive beliefs, optimism, growth mindset, or strength of character. Parents who are not aware of the consequences of their emotions need help understanding why they react in certain ways.

> Over 75% of parents report a moderate to extreme occurrence of grief in the USA (PGV Parent Survey, 2015).
>
> "Most parents are unaware of their emotions, such as stress, and therefore do not seek counsel (Onelia Aybar, Education Director, Dominican Republic)."

Positive psychology does not say we neglect personal challenges, undesirable emotions, or stressful situations. It acknowledges any state of being as an opportunity for self-development. Helping parents understand what causes stress, such as fear or worry, can help caregivers navigate uncertainty or emotional vulnerability.

Parents may not feel comfortable traveling long distances for hearing health services, for example. A new experience may be frightening. Schools with staff who lack training and resources may shun children with disabilities, and parents may not feel competent or equipped emotionally to challenge or talk with school administration about possible solutions. These events can be stressful and emotionally draining. Finding courage, strength, honor, or wisdom to push through these events builds resilience, and supports personal growth and determination to help their children learn.

Choosing to see these emotional events as catalysts for change opens doors to personal growth. Acknowledging and accepting feelings associated with any difficult experience are not only healthy coping strategies but also opportunities to shift the mindset and attitudes. To engage in a positive parenting journey, talking about and exploring feelings are healthy. The hearts of parents need compassionate coaching and support for them to be mindful and aware of feelings that occur and possibly recur.

Emotional awareness can unleash some of the burden parents carry with them and influence how they engage. Once parents grasp an understanding that emotions are central to the nervous system of the body, they may be able to witness when emotions arise and why they react the way they do. The human brain responds to and governs the nervous system of the body; the sympathetic system triggers a rapid heart rate or sweat glands and the parasympathetic system helps our bodies become calm.[26] Balancing the automatic nervous system can help. Hope may trigger possibilities. Fear may prevent engaging behaviors. Worry might spin the mind in confusing directions. By understanding emotions, parents can learn to cope with feelings that hinder participation in decision making and goal-directed behavior.

In 1968, Kubler-Ross first described five stages of emotions people with grief experience: denial, anger, bargaining, depression, acceptance.[27] Practitioners and science continue to evaluate how parental grief triggers feelings associated with children's hearing loss. Denial of children's hearing loss, an avoidance of feelings, and minimization of a delay in the child's language can be seen among many caregivers who are learning to cope with their children's hearing loss. Emotions such as extreme sadness and depression can be immobilizing. Anger stirs the mind's perpetual reasoning to blame, avoids the truth, and pities oneself. Shame is a function of fear or guilt. Cultural beliefs, family pressure, and community ignorance around hearing loss cast shadows of self-doubt. Parents who have low self-esteem and poor self-image are the most at risk. Their response can lead to excessive fear and worrying. This can affect both mind and body in a variety of ways:

- Disrupted sleep
- Headaches
- Difficulty concentrating
- Nausea
- Muscle tension
- Exhaustion
- Irritability
- Elevated levels of the stress hormone, cortisol
- Difficulty making decisions [28]

Attitudes expressed about hearing loss, slander from the community, or blame for the cause of the child's hearing loss affect parents differently. Social stigma is prevalent in many communities and parents must find ways to cope. The mindset and emotional reaction of parents could be based on numerous reasons (e.g.: lack of financial resources, limited or no parental supports). Parents may not have control over their environment or their children's hearing loss, but they can choose how they respond to what people say and how to carry themselves throughout the day. A goal for practitioners can be to help parents transfer emotional reactivity into goal directed energy that supports their well-being and inevitably their children.

Parents will be more able to apply their parenting skills and abilities in support of their children when they understand their feelings and how experiences trigger certain emotions. This can sometimes help parents release judgmental thoughts or develop self-regulation. When parents learn how to gain control over situations that trigger emotional reactivity, they come to accept and let go of emotional burden. They are able to think with reason when they understand that their emotions are normal. They benefit from reminders that emotions are cyclical and can re-emerge in response to changing circumstances.

# EMOTIONAL AWARENESS

Emotional awareness is an ability to understanding feelings. This can help parents learn to navigate, accept, and cope with hearing loss and the challenges they face. Parents must first identify feelings and understand what triggers their emotions. This can also help them regulate emotions and cope with greater responsiveness.

Practitioners can suggest parents take a few moments of quiet introspection. This gives parents permission to observe their current thoughts and feelings. Especially in a challenging situation, parents should take a moment to notice any physical reactions, such as a rapid heartbeat or a face feeling flushed or hot (anger, fear, embarrassment).

Consider the following questions to guide parents' awareness of their emotional response to the situation.

> *When you are with your child, what emotions do you often feel?*
>
> *Do thoughts in your mind dominate the situation and cause you to be distracted?*
>
> *Do your thoughts lead you to worry about your child's future or feelings of isolation?*
>
> *When or how do emotions take control of the way you react or behave?*
>
> *What feelings appear most often when you think about your child's hearing?*
>
> *Have you transformed feelings of worry or fear into something positive in the past?*

# Parent Vision

"Behind every young child who believes in himself is a parent who believed first."
~ Matthew Jacobson

Parents' vision for their children often hinges on their own belief, values, and acceptance of hearing loss. No one can ignore the fact that our personal lives are entangled with personal opinions and experiences. We all come from different cultures and families. Our education, or access to education, varies across the world and within a community. Undeniably we form our beliefs and perceptions based on cultures and knowledge we acquire. And if we are truthful with ourselves, we know that we absorb biases and opinions that come from our learning experiences and exposure to people around us.

For parents to truly be empowered, they need their opinions to be heard. They need their feelings and thoughts to be understood and acknowledged. Practitioners must talk with parents about their insights and desires, even when time is of the essence in their practice. It is imperative to understand how parent emotions impart a vision or goal they have for their children. On a mission trip in India, it was revealed that hundreds of parents were never asked about the vision they have for their children. They held their thoughts and beliefs to themselves because no practitioner had ever considered their views. Parents should always be asked these two important questions:

> *What vision do you have for your child's future?*

> *If your child did not have hearing loss, what would be your vision?*

Parents can awaken to the critical value and importance of their participation at every stage of their children's lives, and this begins with the vision they have for their children, regardless of hearing loss. A practitioner can guide parents to explore their beliefs and perceptions they have. Embracing parents' views and then helping them see positive futures can facilitate their involvement and participation, such as setting goals and embracing their children's potential. When parents envision positive futures for their children, they engage in hope and possibility. Parents want to support their children's development and see them succeed. Working through limiting beliefs may be needed. Beliefs imposed by the culture or the family environment may get in the way of the true desire to see children thrive. And the beliefs parents have, their opinions and attitudes, are passed on to their children. Parents may need help to recognize what limits their thinking in order to embrace a future of opportunity.

# Parent Belief

"At the root of a behavior is a belief." ~ Maria Sorois, PsyD.

Babies come into the world with basic drives such as hunger and thirst; they rapidly learn language and trust in their caregivers. Their personalities are revealed in a short period of time and are influenced by biological markers. As children age, their families and cultures help form their perceptions and attitudes about the world. Traditions are handed down from generation to generation. Beliefs may be imposed. Children grow up, marry, gain life experiences, and live in a world connected to their culture. They may learn that they can choose beliefs rather than conform to attitudes and opinions of others.

Culture plays a significant role in parents' beliefs and response to hearing loss. In some parts of the world, a child with hearing loss is perceived as a sin or a curse. The hearing loss may be attributed to the mother, to the bad blood of a family, or as punishment from God. A family may feel dishonored or exile the child and mother from the home. Some societies look down on hearing loss and disregard any potential of a child who cannot hear or speak. These beliefs sometimes predict how parents respond to their children's hearing loss.

> **Beliefs and Values guide actions and behavior, though there are differences.**
>
> *Beliefs* are assumptions we hold to be true even without proof or evidence. These are assumptions about the world and are often based on culture and religion.
>
> *Values* are principles that motivate us to make decisions. They are moralities that we deem important to our personal character.

A belief often directs how parents nurture their children and engage in their learning and development. Practitioners can have a conversation about the beliefs and perceptions parents have of hearing loss and their children's potential. Though practitioners are not able to control all parent opinions and attitudes, they do have influence and through positive interventions can shift the parents' mindset toward the possibilities of their children and unlimiting beliefs.

Every parent should explore their beliefs, values, and perceptions around hearing loss. Practitioners can help parents identify and express them. In doing so, practitioners might better understand the parent mindset and what might drive positive behavior and parent participation. Factors that affect human behavior include the following: attitudes, perceptions, genetics, culture, social norms and ethics of a society, religious inclination, coercion, and influence by authority.[29]

When parents first learn their children have a hearing loss, and when they have no reference to or experience with hearing health or habilitation, their vision of their children's lives is shattered. The future may feel uncertain and threatened. Though cultures are different, caregivers in low resource environments often receive the same underlying message: disability means a departure from what life is supposed to be. The family equilibrium has suddenly shifted. Life as they know it seems to tilt and waver; stress and worry might seep into caregiver's minds about their children's ability to talk, to become educated, to get a job, or to marry. Fear for the children's future may uproot the vision parents have. These thoughts can lead to feeling depressed, sad, lonely, or stressed.

Practitioners can help parents move beyond any of their existing limiting beliefs. Beliefs ground parents in how they will respond, as well as how they perceive themselves as caregivers. Helping parents explore their beliefs in ways that influence positive and forward-thinking behavior is essential.

> In the pursuit of a rich, meaningful life, there is a growing body of science suggesting that our greatest values guide our behavior. Values are not static; they vary from culture to culture. Values like freedom, honesty, equality, integrity, happiness, wisdom are based on belief. Values are principals a person lives by. What a person thinks or feels about a situation (or themselves) influences how the person behaves and acts. Curiosity, social contact, status, family, power, and honor are some examples of values that can drive behavior.
>
> (Todd B. Kashdan, Ph.D., "16 Ways to Motivate," March 26, 2015, www.creativitypost.com/psychology).

# TRANSFORMING LIMITING BELIEFS

To transform a limiting belief or a stressful situation into a productive engine for positive growth, consider asking questions or reflecting parent beliefs back at them in the form of a question. This strategy can help parents see beliefs more clearly.

1) Acknowledge the parent belief and then get more information.

    *I heard you say ---. How might you see this differently?*

2) Consider asking the following questions to work through negativity:

    *What most worries you?*

    *Are you truly afraid of this?*

    *Does this belief make you feel angry, sad, or happy? If so, why?*

    *How would you act/behave if you did not have this feeling in your mind?*

Allow time for parents to think through their responses. Help them identify reactions that trigger anxiety, worry, feelings of self-doubt, or fear. Help parents reflect on their beliefs, helping them to confront stressful or worrisome events without over-focusing on these. Steer parents toward the possibilities for their children to break limiting beliefs they may have. Express how there are both challenging and joyful moments. The conversation should balance good and bad, sad and happy, and tension and ease. Life is challenging with a child who has a disability, yet there is also joy that is experienced. Supporting the potential of children with hearing loss requires parents remain optimistic as well as realistic.

**NOTE TO PRACTITIONER:**

Furthermore, it can be healthy for parents to reflect on what they might be able to control versus what they might be able to influence. Here are some examples of things they can control:

- emotional reactivity,
- time spent with their child,
- attendance at workshops and parent meetings,
- positive mindset,
- decisions.

Things parents might influence include the following:

- limiting beliefs imposed by others,
- social stigma,
- family perceptions around children's hearing loss and potential.

When parents become aware of the way things truly are, including their emotions, they then often realize they can influence and control many situations. Letting go of things they cannot control occurs when parents fully accept the reality of their situation and acquire freedom to release what may be holding them back.

# Meaning

"Meaning Permeates our Life." ~ Michael Stegar

Janus, the ancient Roman god of beginnings, endings, gates, transitions, and duality has two faces: one which looks to the benefits of the future and one which looks to the complexities of the past. We learn from the past, and the future is often a projection of what we know. Janus also teaches us that conflict can result in inner peace.

When parents struggle with the stigma of disability, minimal services, and the limiting beliefs, it would be natural to project uncertainties into the future. When parents learn to rise to a higher purpose and choose to see their pasts and their journeys as opportunity for growth, meaning can help parents to cope with any challenge and adversity. Challenges can also lead parents to find meaning and a sense of direction.

Parents are often perplexed with a reason why they have a child with hearing loss. "Why me" questions arise internally, and parents struggle to understand the cause of hearing loss. Recognizing and acknowledging these kinds of internal struggles becomes an important step toward a meaningful journey. The cause of their children's hearing loss may never be known, yet past experiences may have taught parents to be resilient and independent.

Parents interpret their social and emotional experiences differently, and they may need to reflect on their purpose or why they have become caregivers of children with hearing loss. Many parents push this notion aside, suppress feelings, and engage in relationships that support their needs without recognition of their grief or stress. Sometimes, knowing the reasons why their children acquire hearing loss can help parents embrace their children with more understanding, compassion, and integrity. Audiologists, hearing health technicians, community rehabilitation coordinators, teachers, speech therapists, and other parents remain key supporters to help parents work through their purpose and roles as caregivers.

"When we align our thoughts, actions, and emotions with the higher parts of ourselves, we are filled with enthusiasm, purpose, and meaning," states Gary Zukav in his book *Seat of the Soul*. Personal power within refers to how we embrace thoughts, beliefs, intentions, and actions. Meaning in one's life can renew energy and vitality in the soul. Purpose gives meaning to life, and this carries a degree of motivation. Having a reason to get up in the morning, such as caring for a child and loved one and getting ready for work, is purposeful.

The transition to a life with children who cannot hear is a new beginning for most parents. This uncertainty can be unsettling for a family who has never experienced hearing loss. Caring for a child with hearing loss is likely something parents know little about, and they might ruminate negatively. An objective and non-judgmental view of how they see themselves in any difficult situation requires a degree of inner strength and will power.

Parents need to find a purpose in the care they give to their children. Though parents may feel completely alone and isolated from other people in their community, having a purpose helps parents build a sense of worth and identity. The internal chaos they experience in their hearts will calm when they discover what matters most and when they feel motivated to engage in the role to help their children learn and communicate.

In other words, meaning directs energies effectively. When caregivers discover how to care for and nurture their children, they often engage more meaningfully in services and supports that they learn from. When basic needs such as love, respect, and emotional security are fulfilled, parents can engage in the needs of their children. Even when these basic needs are threatened, a sense of purpose can help people bounce back. Parents embrace the vision and dreams they have for their children when grounded in purpose. The roots of engagement, therefore, must be linked to events parents can relate to and embrace with interest and focus.

Some caregivers naturally engage with a purpose by teaching their children a vocation and helping them become participants in mainstream society. For example, a mother in Honduras packages and sells spices. She brings her daughter with her daily, intentionally teaching her the business. Her daughter is also talented, and all day long while waiting for customers she paints images onto handbags and other saleable items. The bond they have is strong, and over the years the young girl thrives in her community as an artist. The mother's vocation involves a purpose and engages her child's achievement, regardless of her child's hearing loss.

Having meaning in people's lives shifts their outlook and frame of mind; it can help parents rise to higher levels of self-esteem and peace of mind. The responsibilities in raising children with hearing loss is a new and complex beginning for many caregivers, involving many tasks. Caring for Hearing Assistive Technologies, explaining natural communication, involving children in house chores, reading a book or storytelling, and nurturing children's socio-emotional growth all take time for parents to learn to do and incorporate into their family lives. Children's development depends on their caregivers and the purposeful journey of caregivers who help their children thrive.

## A Note to Practitioner:

Practitioners influence how parents respond to the needs of their children. Parents appreciate when practitioners ask them questions about what they think and believe are important. Parents are integral to the solutions and outcomes sought for their children, and they need to feel connected and valued. Coaching and advice parents receive from practitioners are effective when practitioners lead parents to discover a purpose and internal motivation that engages them in learning and in hearing health and habilitation practices.

Purpose and meaning can be fostered when parents engage in services that help their children. Practitioners can consider parents' routines and ensure everyday jobs align with the hearing and language goals they envision for these children. Parents may or may not put into practice the hearing health and habilitation lessons that are explained to them; thus, practitioners can reflect on such questions as:

> *Are parents integrating suggestions for language and learning with feelings of optimism, meaning, and purpose?*
>
> *Are parent beliefs and the future vision of the child aligned with these lessons?*

# STRESS IS NOT A BAD THING

"Stress is a function of the view you take of events." ~ Ellen Langer

The extent to which parents are experiencing stress and grief influences how they engage and interact with their children. Parents cope in different ways, and they need help navigating their journeys as caregivers of children with hearing loss. Parent supports and counsel are greatly needed.[30] Informational supports help parents understand hearing health, their children's hearing loss, and choices parents have in available services. Importantly, supports help parents cope with challenging and stressful situations.

Parenting in general can be a demanding experience; parenting a child with a sensory or developmental disability that you know nothing about can be even more challenging. Hearing health, PGV mission experiences, and parent survey results imply the majority of parents of children with hearing loss experience stress, regardless of the education and socio-economic status of the families. Reports on moderate to severe degrees of parental stress range from 44% to over 75%.

> Stress release is linked to benefit finding experiences. This "benefit finding" refers to positive psychological change that is experienced from adversity and other challenges and helps people rise to a higher level of functioning (*Encyclopedia of Positive Psychology, 2009*).

In developing countries parents are often consumed with their economic well-being, such as finding employment. Taking care of other children in the home, putting food on the table, gathering water, and attending to house chores adds to the "to do" list. Hearing health and habilitation of children can be an overwhelming addition to parents' daily survival and family obligations. Most parents in developing countries do not deny they experience stress when discussed. However, many are immersed in multiple needs and are not aware that *stress is a factor that diminishes their capacity for proper parenting of their children*. As a consequence, families may not seek, nor are offered, the support they need.

Research points to the fact that poverty and levels of economic resources affect parental stress.[31] It is also estimated that 50% of women who are depressed during and after pregnancy are not diagnosed and treated, even though 80% report begin comfortable with the idea of screening.[32/33] Providing supports that help parents reduce the risk of stress, grief, and depression is critical. Social supports given to caregivers are likewise associated with decreased psychological distress in children.[34] (Supports are discussed in Part Three.)

Parents in low resource communities are often unaware of their stress and emotional grief triggered by their children's hearing loss. They more likely associate stress with sadness, and parents of children with hearing loss throughout the Dominican Republic and India had difficulty identifying or talking about stress and other emotions in their lives. When stress and the varying nature of emotions are explained, parents with whom PGV has met more confidently express their personal challenges. Doubt, sadness, anxiety, and guilt over their children's hearing loss differ among parents and depend on the circumstance. Fluctuating emotions are common and can cause varying degrees of burden on parents. Many parents are relieved to know other parents experience similar distress. Their stories interrelate.

Stress, grief, depression, or fear about the future can also distract parents from responding to their children's social, emotional, and cognitive development. Parents might avoid responding to their children's needs. They may even minimize any problem exists. We know that appropriate supports can help parents rise to higher levels of achievement.

More often, parents with higher levels of education and who are more resourceful accurately identify with their feelings and degrees of stress. These parents may express anxiety, yet they remain engaged in hearing habilitation and empowered to manage their children's learning, communication, and development. Parents in this population are more likely to confront their feelings. In the face of many challenges, parents are resilient and respond to the needs of their children by acting upon desired goals.

Families in lower resources communities, however, rely more heavily on educators and other practitioners to fix their child's hearing. They may hide their stress or push feelings aside. Even when practitioners inform parents about the hearings aids and ways to communicate with their children, the responsibilities to care for a child with hearing loss may be overwhelming for parents. Distress gets in the way of properly addressing the learning and communication needs of children. Parents need to grow into the comfortable role of caregiver, and with good coaching and relatable information parents can learn to cope with and care for their children with confidence and more assurance.

Stress is not something we want to dwell on, but it is something we can learn from. Psychologists have demonstrated stress that one encounters with life's most challenging moments can lead to positive change.[35] A study by Goodley and Tregaskis states that many parents respond to the emotional and caregiving stressors associated with childhood disability with positive coping and resiliency.[36] In other words, stress does not have to be a bad thing when parents learn to cope and understand the nature of their emotions. There is an incredible release of tension once parents understand stress and become aware of their feelings and thoughts associated with stressful situations.

# Resilience

"At the root of resilience is positive emotion, optimism, ability to adapt to change."
~ Maria Sirois, PsyD

Resilience is an ability to overcome adversity, trauma, tragedy, threats, or stress.[37] Poverty, health, disability and employment, for example, are common challenges that caregivers face in low resource communities. Being receptive to difficult experiences and open to embrace innermost feelings and thoughts can help. There is a choice to see hardships, suffering, and pressure of life as experiences to learn from. Bouncing back means being open to possibility and seeing negative events as opportunities for personal growth.

Resilience is cultivated, and everyone at any time or any age has an ability to become more resilient.[38] Over a life span, resilience inevitably shapes the way people respond to life's events, and this dynamic process contributes to healthy human development. Adversity can build a person's resilience and open doors to personal growth.

Qualities commonly found in resilient people include the following:

- Social competence (responsiveness, cultural flexibility, empathy, caring, communication skills, and a sense of humor);
- Problem-solving (planning, help-seeking, critical and creative thinking);
- Autonomy (a sense of identity, self-efficacy, self-awareness, task-mastery, and adaptive distancing from negative messages and conditions);
- Sense of purpose and belief in a bright future (goal direction, educational aspirations, optimism, faith, and spiritual connectedness).[39]

Resilience is complex and factors that can help improve one's ability to endure life's inevitable challenges and adapt to change involve several approaches to well-being. Such interventions considered in this resource include mindfulness, leadership, character strengths, and parent supports. Resilience is grounded on personal growth and capacity building. A global report on resilience indicates six factors that increase resilience (2018):

- Assertiveness
- Decisiveness
- Focus
- Fulfillment
- Optimism
- Presence [40]

The report furthers discusses how resilience in parts of Asia, The Americas, and Europe is an important determinant of productivity, emotional intelligence, and well-being. "Resilience is a foundational psychological tool which empowers the individual to feel capable of handling uncertainty," states Bradley Hook, contributor to The Resilience Institute.[41] Dr. Maria Sorois also states, "Resilience resides in our capacity to honor our suffering, respect our needs for self-care, and shape each day toward a braver, more authentic, and more inspiring future."[42] She proclaims how resilience is mandatory in life and is crucial to a thriving life. To develop resiliency, she suggests the following four strategies:

1. Focus on the positive (page 35-38)
2. Know your strengths (Part Two)
3. Try "benefit finding" (page 39)
4. Practice gratitude (pages 39-42)

Mentioned previously, parents living in low- and limited- resources communities are often resilient. They face hardships and adversity every day. Caregivers of children with hearing loss have opportunities to learn from and nurture the path of resilience. Finding joy, being grateful, embracing optimism, and knowing one's strengths increase capacity to rebound from uncertain circumstances. Resilient caregivers confront their most painful realities and persevere through difficult times when they apply the four strategies above. When they remain empathetic, flexible, optimistic, and goal oriented they gain resilience. A parent's knowledge of their skills and strengths further motivates parents to engage in their lives with determination. The vision parents have for their children with hearing loss depends on their sustained participation. When parents intentionally foster positivity and growth mindsets, they open doors to their ability to reach for the goals they seek for their children. Further, being mindfully aware of their character strengths, parents build capacity and innate potential. Character strengths are empowering. Discussed in detail in Part Two, they are known to strengthen human resilience.[43]

*Give yourself permission to be human. When we accept emotions – such as fear, sadness or anxiety – as natural, we are more likely to overcome them. Rejecting our emotions, positive or negative, can lead to frustration and unhappiness.* ~ Tal Ben-Shahar

# ASSESS YOUR RESILIENCE

Assess your resilience by completing the following exercise. Take time to reflect on a ***challenging or adverse situation***. What questions run through your mind, heart, body, and spirit? This self-awareness exercise may help you to define physical, emotional, and spiritual principles that contribute to how well you bounce back from challenging situations. It may help you grow with new perspective.

Heart (emotions/feelings)

Mind (learning/thoughts)

Body (physical sensations)

Spirit (belief, faith, values)

# COPING WITH HEARING LOSS

Caregivers experience a range of emotions over the care given to their children with hearing loss. They may be unsure of how to get help or how to plan for their children's future. They may compare their children to children who hear and speak. They may fear they have no control or support to help manage aspects of their children's development. Their emotions may be riddled with perceptions of hearing loss and the vision they had for their children before diagnosis. Parents cope with hearing loss differently. Coping is a natural mechanism and helps parents deal with emotional difficulties that arise.

Early knowledge of hearing loss can unload some of the emotional burden parents experience. Parents feel less stress when they are equipped with an understanding of their children's needs. Knowledge facilitates the ways parents cope and manage their children's hearing loss. Over time, parents feel less anxiety and worry. They are more inclined to engage in strategies that support their children's development when given supports that help their children communicate and learn.

> Forward thinkers, optimists, and problem solvers of the world often find solutions in difficult situations. Hope drives positive change, and conflicts are overcome by taking actionable and confident steps (Davis et al., 1998; Janoff-Bulman and Frantz, 1997).

It is hard to manage hearing loss when resources and parent supports are limited. Parents feel overwhelmed by an unpredictable future, especially when they have no knowledge or support. Even when parents feel they have little control or are burdened with stigma of hearing loss, they love their children. Kindness, forgiveness, and perspective are character strengths that can help parents accept their situation and cope the best way possible.

Hope and optimism play a key role in a parent's ability to manage hearing loss and support their children. Hope is an emotion and is the "expectation of something desired, or a desire combined with expectation" (Oxford English Dictionary). Having hope does not necessarily mean caregivers explicitly engage and facilitate their children's learning and communication, but it can lead to a desire for solutions and services that support their children. Hope is associated with optimism, which is a core belief. It is a certainty that good results and positive outcomes will occur. Many parents are aware of the need to focus their energy by being optimistic. They express the importance of thinking positively. They have faith in God or know that if they pray for help it will arrive. This coping mechanism helps parents put things into perspective.

Separating the hearing loss from the child is important. The child with hearing loss is a child first; the hearing loss is a condition and is not the whole child. This realization alone can be helpful to parents. Even when parents embrace their children with love and acceptance, knowing their children's hearing loss does not define their children helps them cope.

## *Observations in the developing world*

Parents accrue beliefs that may be limiting or untrue. Children who are delayed in their speech and language present such misinterpreted beliefs about their intelligence. Community perceptions of hearing loss are often based on the social environment, and the ability for parents to cope is often tainted by opinions coming from family and their community. Some cultures see hearing loss as compromising to human potential, while others see deafness as a gift. There may be people in the community and within the family structure who are disrespectful of children with differences. Abuse can be unbearable to witness. Stigma can be so harsh in low resource communities that caregivers might think hearing loss is a curse or a punishment.

Further, denial of hearing loss may center on a belief that "nothing is wrong," despite hearing about a diagnosis or a speculation to the contrary. Parents often minimize the hearing loss and believe their children comprehend everything, especially when their children wear Hearing Assistive Technologies (HAT). Unintentionally, parents hinder their children's communication and development when they cannot cope with the realities of hearing loss or their children's delay.

When caregivers become aware of their perceptions around hearing loss, as well as any limiting belief, they may be able to let go of negative views and beliefs. Coping strategies matter because limited beliefs of children's potential thwart or delay parents' active participation in the children's learning, which can hinder the children's progress. Finding ways to cope also helps boost parents' acceptance of their situation and their critical role in helping their children. Ultimately, all parents want to express more love and kindness toward their children.

To deepen the ways parents cope, parents need to hear or see examples of children who succeed. Stories about a challenging situation that a family overcame can be helpful. Parents need to know that children with hearing loss can thrive like other children in their community and examples of ways children succeed in school, at work, and in their communities support the parent vision for their children's future. Bringing light to a situation often dissolves parent anxiety and worry. When parents have someone to help them navigate hearing loss in positive ways, they are more inclined to engage in ways that help their children. Parents' ability to cope with hearing loss may hinder a positive vision they have for their children.

When parents acquire knowledge, instill hope and possibility, and find positive supports to help them, they gain assurance and feel more empowered to help their children. However, *coping begins as an inside job*. Parents need to believe in themselves and their journeys. When parents are aware of their internal struggles, their emotional experiences, and the beliefs that accrue, they can put into perspective ways to cope and set intentions. The strategies mentioned below are a few ways parents learn to cope with problems, get support, and perhaps find purpose.

> "Cultivation of mindfulness, engagement, positive emotions, vital involvement, relationships, meaning, accomplishment, practicing gratitude, and experiencing flow increase our capacity for positivity as well as resilience" (Schmidt, Positive Psychology Summit, 2017).

# Four Coping Strategies:
## Mindfulness, Meditation, Introspection, Self-care

### I. Mindfulness

"To be mindful, focusing on process over outcome allows free rein to intuition and creativity, and opens us to new information and perspective." ~ Ellen Langer

Mindfulness can be a helpful coping strategy for parents of children with hearing loss and facilitate well-being. Jon Kabat Zinn states, "Mindfulness is awareness that arises through paying attention, on purpose, in the present moment, and non-judgmentally." The practice also involves being curious, open, and accepting of experiences. Mindfulness is an approach to observing everything that comes into the present moment: sensory experiences of sight, hearing, touch, taste, and smell, seeing things as they truly are. Practicing mindfulness can facilitate ways parents cope with their journeys and embrace their children's needs with clear attention and intention. Being aware of present moments and accepting things as they are is known to enhance psychological well-being.

Mindfulness includes noticing the thoughts that arise in the mind. It begins by being aware of when the mind wanders and catching thoughts that project into the future or dwell upon the past. Many holistic practitioners view mindfulness as a way to feel stable in the mind, see clarity of the situation, and allow wisdom and intuition to arise. Being present to experiences encourages the mind to focus and slows the tendency of the mind to wander.

Both eastern philosophy and western medicine recognize the value of paying attention to the present moment, rather than ruminating on the past or getting pulled into the mind's thoughts. Mindfulness has been practiced for over 2,500 years, and it begins with simple awareness and centering of the mind and body in the present moment. According to the Buddha, three ways to establish mindfulness begins with the awareness of breath and the sensation of breath in the body, the noticing of sensations that are pleasant, unpleasant or neutral in the body, and the observation of *citta*, a Sanskrit word referring to perceptions and mental processes found within the workings of the human mind.[44] A focus on breathing helps calm the body's nervous system and train the brain to arrive in the moment. The practice involves expanding awareness to the environment and beholding the world around without judgement or critique.

Mindfulness is a process, not a destination.

By remaining in the present moment, mindfulness grounds one in truth and reality. Consciously choosing to observe the present by focusing on the task at hand and witnessing any sensation that arises, can prevent the mind from wandering or rumination. The brain is an amazing organ that processes thoughts and experiences that shape perceptions. It can revisit thoughts over and over again and hold on to memories. Allowing the mind to steer away from reality can invoke an untruth or an unhappiness in one's life, yet when mindfulness is mastered it can lead to feelings of peace, calm, and acceptance. The practice facilitates seeing what is real and reducing energy given to what is not.

Being a witness to the present moment is like being aware of being aware! It necessitates paying attention to every instant, every experience. It entails noting whatever arises without critique and analysis. Mindfulness means being a witness to the details of the shadows, steps taken along a path or road, or the splash of water filling a bucket. Each moment is a unique and separate experience. Paying attention to the particulars while doing chores or the movements and speech of people are also opportunities to become mindful and present. Being attentive to noises in the city, the sensory experiences of food, or the tranquility experienced in the countryside are still more examples of ways to pay close attention.

There is a growing number of mental health counselors and practitioners who call upon mindfulness to foster psychological well-being, especially the ability to improve concentration and clarity of thoughts. The practice of mindfulness can lead a person to greater emotional balance, happiness, and compassion, as well as reduce levels of stress, depression, anxiety, and interpersonal problems. There has been an explosion of research in psychotherapy and positive effect of mindfulness (Baer, 2003; Greeson, 2009; Grossman, Niemann, Schmidt, & Walach, 2004; Keng, Smoski, Robins, 2011). Many benefits include lowering stress levels, reducing anxiety, and improving immune function.[45] The holistic practice over thousands of years has now become mainstream in many societies.

Research has also found that mindfulness facilitates well-being and benefits emotional regulation.[46] The practice has positive effects on the conscious mind. Because minds are active and thousands of thoughts occur every day, staying in the moment requires concentration and curiosity. A regular practice of mindfulness helps a person remain conscious of experiences and thus focus on what is real and present, versus what is not. Being mindful helps people build self-regulation and cope with the chaos and struggle.

Integrating a mindfulness practice into the day requires an understanding of being aware and watchful. It involves noticing the moments when one is doing something completely different from what the mind is thinking. Once understood, people can adapt mindfulness in their lives in any situation. Based on many studies, benefits to mindfulness practice include the following:

- Reduced rumination
- Stress reduction
- Improved focus
- Improved relationship
- Reduced emotional reactivity
- Cognitive flexibility

## A Note to Practitioner:

The conscious mind is an important element of health and well-being. It can improve relationships, foster competence in life's endeavors, build a richness and connection to experiences, and alleviate comparisons to others.[47] If we transfer this concept to parents who struggle and grieve over their children's hearing loss, we can help parents accept life as it is given to them, disability or no disability, and use mindfulness practice to help free caregivers from clutter that pervades the mind or prevents them from engaging with their children. Moments caring for their children are enjoyed more when parents are attentive to their children. The responsibilities and role as caregiver may seem less burdensome as a result. Being present in the journey, and embracing all that life offers, is to enter it with acceptance and empathy.

Practitioners can introduce mindfulness to parents and encourage they notice their experiences - what they see, hear, feel, and think. Being mindful can help parents attune to their intuition as well as feelings of connectedness, focus, and calm. Mindfulness can be practiced anywhere: during a community event, doing chores, walking along a path, working. Encourage parents to practice mindfulness daily. Here are steps to get started:

1. Ask parents to take several deep breaths and relax their shoulders, jaw, and body.

2. Next, have them focus on the present situation by noticing the feeling and sensation of breath in the whole body.

3. Finally, ask parents to expand their awareness to the immediate environment. What details do they notice? Can they note what feels pleasant or unpleasant?

Parents can practice mindfulness in a variety of ways. Several disciplines promote mindfulness, such as yoga, tai chi, and meditation. Moments when parents can practice mindfulness include washing dishes or listening to a friend. Reassure parents that as they increasingly practice mindfulness, they may come to notice what they are missing; they may realize how often the mind wanders away from the present.

Further, mindfulness can help parents remain attentive to their children's environment and experiences. Through mindfulness, parents can become more aware of subtle actions their children make with their eyes, hands, body, and face. Parents will attend to moment-to-moment needs, helping their children explore and learn. The opportunities for their children to learn increase when parents attune to every moment they have with their children and engage in their children's world. Mindfulness helps parent feel connected, calm, and focused.

> "Feelings come and go like clouds in a windy sky.
>
> Conscious breathing is my anchor." - *Thich Nhat Hanh*

# MINDFUL BREATHING EXERCISE

This Breathing Exercise is just one example of how to jump-start a mindfulness routine. It is a practice in relaxing the body and being aware of breath sensations. Awareness and focus on breathing promote mindfulness because when the body and the mind settle, there is psychological space for building moment-to-moment watchfulness. A regular practice helps stimulate the para-sympathetic system and balance the body's nervous system. Balancing mind and body are key to controlling our emotions and calming our fight or flight response.

The experience of concentrating on the breath, feeling sensations of breath in the body, and observing thoughts is a practice. After three-five minutes of mindful breathing, parents report feeling more relaxed and calmer in the mind. They are often able to return to a task, decision making, and needs of their family with more focus. The suggested script below is one way to focus on the present moment experience of breathing, while also shifting mindsets toward positive self-regard.

> "Take a pause and find a comfortable seat in a chair or on the ground; you can sit against a wall if this helps. Choose a quiet place if possible. Allow your hands to rest gently on your lap. Allow your body to come to stillness and relax your shoulders and jaw.
>
> Close your eyes and focus on your breathing – both the inhales and exhales. As you come to an awareness of the breath, mindfully observe and feel the sensation of oxygen moving into and out of the nostrils. Notice how *breathing in* fills your rib cage and lifts your heart. When you exhale, try to relax even more. Find a natural rhythm to your breathing and observe the breath sensations.
>
> As you fill your body with oxygen, envision filling a clear glass with water, and then empty the glass as you exhale. Let every inhale fill you with the essence of life and positive energy. Perhaps you say to yourself with every inhale, "I am joy" or "I am happy." As you breathe out, say to yourself "calm mind, calm mind" and repeat this with every breath. Choose any mantra or motto that feels affirming, for example "I feel peace in my body" or "I make myself twice as relaxed with every exhale."

## II. Meditation

"**The best and most beautiful things in this world cannot be seen or even heard, but must be felt with the heart.**" ~ Helen Keller

Meditation is best described as a state of being, and there is no right or wrong way to meditate. It is a practice that encourages relaxation and a slowing down of the mind and its rampant thoughts. Meditation is a path to mindfulness, and a meditative experience can be a simple awareness and acceptance of thoughts and body sensations. One can sit, stand, or walk mindfully with focused attention on the present moment. One can stare at an object such as a plant or the horizon to improve concentration. Meditation can be guided or unguided. It is a practice of observing experiences that come and go without judgement, critique, or analysis.

Meditation has its roots in Hindu traditions; theologians and philosophers from centuries ago proclaimed its many benefits. A regular practice helps relax the nervous system of the body and can free the mind from entanglements and hindrances that blind the heart. A regular practice reduces blood pressure and stress, and it increases a healthy lifestyle and self-awareness. It can improve cognitive skills and concentration.[48] Meditation creates psychological space for clear knowing (wisdom) and reflection (self-discovery). Rather than getting caught up in thought or emotions, creating psychological space can loosen layers of emotional grief, suffering, and limiting beliefs. It can lead to seeing and acting upon clear intentions. Used for thousands of years in eastern philosophy, meditation is the inroad to awakening consciousness, and in quiet moments we can get to know ourselves better.

Meditation can guide parents toward happier journeys in the care they give to their children. Parents are busy, and they may struggle with day-to-day economic hardship, lack of support, and stigma of hearing loss. Being in silence with the mind and body can give parents an opportunity to witness and observe what is actually going on. Minds often wander away from reality, analyze, and plan. Bodies can be fatigued or filled with tension. Meditating creates space in the mind and relaxes the body. It is an opportunity to move away from logic and tension to peace in the mind and the body. Rather than getting caught up in "doing," meditation can help parents "be."

Further, mediation can help people to connect to their innate love. When the mind and the heart connect, an increased sense of wholeness is cultivated. Moving toward heart centeredness helps in all aspects of living. Research shows that humans are happiest when they are giving, sharing, helping, and providing real connection and love to others. Love is a fundamental emotion for all people. It is the greatest gift we can give to others. When we emanate love, we offer it to others. When we embody love, we help ourselves to heal. Pure love flows and is a character strength in all humans.

Parents may be so busy loving others that they may forget to love themselves. Bringing love into the heart can help free parents from their hardships, fears of parenting a child with hearing loss, or worries. They may need to take a few moments to reset their minds and hearts and be reminded there is no need for judgement or shame. These things may take away from their personal power to make good decisions, and to care for self.

Parents can find their own ways to relax the body and create psychological clarity to help them nurture peaceful minds and love for themselves. Prayer, chanting, or performing ritualistic dance are also practices that promote relaxation and transcendent experiences. Parents need to practice whatever makes them feel love and happiness.

## A GUIDED MEDITATION PRACTICE

Parents often focus their love on others and forget how important it is to love themselves. Meditating and focusing on love for 10 minutes can help. Ask parents to close their eyes or soften their gaze on something that is not distracting. They can focus on their breathing and use the breath as a tool for relaxation and coming to the present moment. Should their minds drift away in thoughts or get absorbed in a story, ask parents to return to an awareness of the breath.

Guide parents to a quiet space of loving acceptance. When they breathe in ask them to say to themselves, "I am love." and "I am kind." Ask them to turn away from judgment or self-doubt. Say, "Let go of anything that does not serve you well on the exhale." Remind parents to be self-compassionate and to accept their thoughts with kindness. Parents can breathe in thoughts of health and happiness. Suggest they quietly repeat any mantra that fills them with goodness and truth: "I am worthy." "I am peaceful." "I am happy." "I am love."

During meditation, parents can ask their higher self to connect to their hearts. When they breathe in peace, love, kindness, and gratitude, their hearts can then allow love to permeate throughout their entire bodies.

## III. Introspection

"Only the person who is relaxed can create, and to that mind, ideas flow like lightning."
~ Cicero

Introspection involves self-examination of conscious thoughts, emotions, and mood (wikepedia.org). It is a form of mindfulness and can be a productive practice for positive growth and coping. Tiresome days of caregiving can be daunting, and introspection is a process that can help parents reflect on thoughts and emotional triggers, harnessing a greater capacity to become aware of the mind's divisive ways or imagination.

The introspective approach referred to here is called *metacognition*: becoming a witness to and observing thoughts that pop into the mind (and the feelings around them). We learn from the practice of metacognition that we are not our thoughts. How can we *be* our thoughts when *something else* is making the observation? Metacognition helps people monitor thoughts and gives space for making sense of life experiences.

Becoming aware of the minds pervasive chatter is a practice that can help parents cope with their realities. Thoughts can consume the mind. While estimates differ, experts claim humans average 30,000 thoughts per day; some estimates are as high as 60,000. Regardless of the exact number, the mind never sleeps, and it often wanders. The mind might judge, think about what went wrong rather than right, ruminate over things needing improvement. The mind might wonder about the past or future successes. Rather than get carried away by rising and falling tides of emotion and thought, this practice helps to slow the mind and regulate mood. Metacognition creates the opportunity to develop psychological space needed to calm an emotional, irrational, or erratic mind. Such space is needed to sort through what is real and what is imagined.

Metacognition also affects the way people set goals, adapt, and perform. Once people gain control of their emotional response to thoughts in the mind, there is psychological space for positive learning and decision making. Energy can be directed toward a purpose. The goal of metacognition is to create independent learners who are cognizant of their own thinking and learning and learn for life.[49]

When parents are introspective, they reflect on their feelings and thoughts. Attending to feelings and intuition enhances personal learning and supports creative problem solving.[50] When parents have insight to their emotions and thoughts, they become aware of how these influence the way they interact with others and their children. Parents may learn fear is a reason why they seek help, or they may notice how they run away from support because of guilt. They may be able to self-examine ways they trust in practitioner suggestions that help their child learn and communicate.

They may become aware of how personal thoughts and wishful thinking do not help their children progress; necessary action steps are required.

Parents can become aware of the mind's power to set traps that can steer them away from helping their children. How does the mind think when parents confront challenges at home and in their communities? Clutter can pervade the mind of a parent who has a child with hearing loss.

Examples of this include:

- Anger about negative perceptions of hearing loss;
- Past experiences that prevent trust in others;
- Fear of the child's future;
- Debilitating sadness and depression about the child's hearing loss that make it nearly impossible for parents to see beyond the fog that shrouds them;
- Limiting beliefs such as "I'm not a good enough parent" or "My child will never be included in my community."

As a strategy for coping with hearing loss, introspection can help parents notice adverse thoughts and reject the mind's propensity to wander into emotional darkness. Can anger, fear, or worry become objects of observation rather than the subjects that are consuming? Parents can shift negative thoughts to appreciation and gratitude. What productive lessons can be learned by recalling positive experiences? Does a neighbor's helping hand to feed or clothe children teach compassion?

Parent minds and hearts must be free of distractions that hinder progress and find psychological space to attend to their children's hearing, learning, and communication needs. Parents will see things more clearly when they get rid of unnecessary clutter in the mind. They may find creative ways to integrate newfound knowledge or build better, closer, and more meaningful connections with others. Parents will grow in new ways once they become aware of thoughts, feelings, or behaviors. When parents examine the mind and heart with self-compassion, they cultivate respect for themselves and others, and their relationships with their children and practitioners can improve.

There is nothing more stimulating than to witness the world through a different lens. It takes courage to get to know oneself and one's actions without being self-critical or egotistical. When the mind is clear or free of these hindrances, people can free themselves from the grip of worry, fear, shame, or inertia and allow their intuition to emerge.

# IV. Self-Care

"Our bodies are our gardens to which our wills are gardeners."
~ William Shakespeare

Self-care is another coping strategy for parents. Parents need encouragement to carve out time for self-care or "feel-good" routines. The responsibilities to care for children with hearing loss makes life busy and physically draining. Many parents, including those in low resources communities, have poor self-esteem and are immersed in shame, guilt, and grief. They neglect self-care as a way to improve their well-being. Self-care and healthy practices require conscious effort and might add time to parents' daily routines. Self-care comes in many forms, such as taking time with friends to laugh, collecting shells on a beach with a child, or going for nature walks to observe beauty. What works for one parent may differ from what works for another. Parents need to do things they love and balance these activities with challenges they encounter with their children and their children's hearing loss. Carving out a little space and time for self-care amid all the pressures and challenges of parenting is essential.

Not surprisingly, results from the Partners for a Greater Voice (PGV) Parent Education Survey (2014) say caregivers often put the needs of their children before their own. More than 44% of caregivers report having no time to care for themselves.

Parents can consider all factors of well-being, and finding natural ways to weave self-care into each day should become an important component. When asked, a majority of parents in developing countries chose talking with others as a primary self-care activity. Here are examples of self-care that parents of children with hearing loss chose in the PGV Parent Education Survey (2014).

- Exercising (cardio)
- Doing Yoga
- Meditating
- Praying
- Eating right/good diet
- Talking with others
- Reading a book
- Sleeping

Practicing mindfulness, physical exercise, yoga, meditation, and gratitude contribute to greater mental and physical well-being (Lutz, Dunne, & Davidson, 2007). For example, meditation improves emotional regulation and leads to good decision-making. Mindfulness can promote connectedness with people and foster happiness. Cardio exercise is healthy for the heart. Mind-body practitioners validate many self-care practices as facilitators of well-being. A consistent practice of good nutrition, exercise, and sleep are now scientifically proven to support the following:

- lowering blood pressure
- improving immunity
- increasing energy
- improving clarity of mind/coherence
- opening oneself to ideas and cognitive flexibility
- reducing depression
- increasing creativity and productivity [51]

## 5% MORE EXERCISE:

**A**sk parents what they would choose for self-care, even beyond the list written above. Suggest taking 5% of a day to weave in a self-care practice every day for a month. This is equivalent to about thirty to forty-five minutes each day. Rather than dive into a full-fledged workout, or hours of practice in yoga or reading, remind parents that taking time 5% of every day for self-care can be beneficial.

Science tells us that if we practice doing something consistently for 30 days or more, it likely becomes a habit. Rewiring the brain in response to behavior can becomes naturally embedded when the behavior is practiced consistently. However, research points out that the more difficult the activity, the longer it can take to affect the area of the brain where habit is formed (basal ganglia). It can take anywhere from 18 to 254 days to instill a new habit.[52] Persistence and consistency of self-care is important, and even if done for 5% of each day.

Parents can also practice Positive Visualization, Moments of Joy, Self-Compassion, Mindful Breathing, and Meditation. They need to decide on a self-care approach that works best and can be easily woven into their day.

# Positive Change

"You must learn a new way to think before you can master a new way to be."
~ Marianne Williamson

Life's accomplishments no doubt ebb and flow like the long or steep trails and ridges of the highest mountain or highland. Sometimes a path is easy to hike, while other paths are challenging or even dangerous. Confronting any indefinite circumstance requires trust in each step, and a belief that we can navigate the path of rock, steepness, or distance. We either get stuck in a rut or we take steps to move forward. It takes perspective and bravery to work through fear that holds us from engaging in life or new possibilities. It takes perseverance and hope to walk miles for a hearing test or to a school for the deaf.

Having a child with disabilities is traumatic. Shame, abuse, and neglect are forms of trauma. In many places around the world, community stigma and perceptions of hearing loss impose false accusations, limiting beliefs, and guilt. Parents often endure such trauma and grief; they may be unaware of how it affects their parenting. Fathers might flee their marriages. Mothers might feel helpless or dejected when they are told they are the cause of their child's hearing loss. Emotional trauma can lead parents to avoid their realities, and they may need help to overcome feelings of *helplessness*, a term coined by Martin Seligman that describes how people are conditioned to avoid painful and adverse situations. Rather than giving up or neglecting what hinders their achievement, parents may need to engage in positive growth that helps them overcome their grief and adversity.

Parents need to become aware of trauma, thoughts that may weigh them down, or relationships that are hindering. Routines that promote positive change can help. We refer to this as positive neural-rewiring. According to research in positive psychology, self-care experiences such as exercise, gratitude practice, doing things you love, and eating healthy are known to reduce stress, decrease the chance of mental and physical ailment, boost productivity, and inspire feelings of happiness. Parents need to feel good and confident as caregivers of children with hearing loss. They may need to change their routines and feelings of helplessness. When parents do things they are good at, or even when they think with positivity, they boost their morale and change the circuitry of their brains. Practitioners can

> The ability of the brain to rewire itself is called *neuroplasticity*. Rewiring the brain requires changing behaviors and thoughts. New experiences are needed to stimulate change. Establishing new routines and taking time for self-care can influence transformation and are known to change the circuitry of the brain (Norman Doidge, MD, *The Brain that Changes Itself*, 2007).

consider the following techniques to foster parents' positivity and to help them rewire negative events stored in the brain:

- using visualization techniques that portray positive parenting experiences
- giving examples of a child's success, regardless of hearing loss
- sharing ways parents remain positive in light of stress or stigma
- telling stories about how parents overcome challenges at home

With thousands of thoughts generated in any given day, the mind can be our worst enemy at times. According to neuroscience, the mind's propensity to think (or overthink) can trigger anxiety and depression.[53] Repeated emotional experiences and thoughts can become engrained in the brain. Often, we fall into traps that lead to second-guessing our intuition or to negative self-talk. A constant bombardment of worrying and fearful thoughts can get in the way of purpose or achievement. It can hinder learning and growth. Coping strategies previously mentioned can help overcome difficult and stressful experiences.

Positive growth for many parents involves shifting away from the hurt to what is good and possible. They often need help to establish healthy mindsets, feel inspired, and become forward thinking. A daily dose of self-compassion and gratitude can help parents approach their day and their relationships with clear, happier minds, thus allowing the cycle of positivity to continue. And when parents cultivate self-compassion and confront feelings of stress, worry, or fear they learn to cope better and overcome adversity.

## PRACTICING SELF-COMPASSION

The practice of self-compassion supports kindness toward oneself and empathy. It supports ways to learn how to overcome shame created by stigma or trauma. When parents truly acknowledge traumatic events, they begin the healing process. Parents are able to experience the following when they practice self-compassion:[54]

- Accept compassion from others
- Learn to be deeply kind toward yourself
- Understand why you have acted out in negative and/or unhealthy ways
- Stop blaming yourself for being the cause of hearing loss
- Forgive yourself
- Create a nurturing inner voice to replace the critical inner voice

# Learning and Development

Life's journey contains lessons that often appear serendipitously. Opportunities to learn are on nearly every path we travel. We might wander into dense forests, only to explore how to navigate the thicket and push through to a safer opening. We might experience self-doubt or anxiety, only to realize how thoughts trigger these emotions. We might walk into a room of people talking about a hearing loss, which can awaken the responsibilities of parenting.

Any major change in life can be scary or unpleasant: a health emergency, loss of job, identifying your child has a disability. Parents who first learn their children can't hear need time to process what this means in their lives. Having a child with a hearing loss might upset the family equilibrium; work schedules, social interactions, schooling, and medical and hearing health needs are all disrupted. More attention may be given to these children, and parents need time to adapt to new terrain and learn how to balance daily routines with the needs of children with hearing loss. An ability to cope with their children's hearing loss is a new personal beginning in many ways. Their journeys come with new responsibilities and learning opportunities that must find space in their lives.

Learning is vital to well-being and essential for personal growth. On one hand, parents need perspective on their children's futures and possibilities. They need to understand what they will face and the roles they will assume. They need encouragement and to know they are capable of parenting children with hearing loss. On the other hand, parents need informational and social supports that help them engage in their children's welfare. They must learn how to engage in their children's communication development and progress and learn new skills. It takes time for parents to grow and learn how to care for their children.

"When you overcome a difficult situation or see it as an opportunity, you learn and grow from the experience. When optimism and self-compassion are applied, the experience, challenge, or perhaps a failure can be personally worthwhile or more meaningful" (Tal Ben-Shahar).

First learning about a child's hearing loss can muddle parent brains with confusing and conflicting information. There is an expansive world within hearing health and language development. The social, emotional, and cognitive needs of children with hearing loss are vast and often different. It is overwhelming for most parents to think of the laundry list of responsibilities they assume in the care they give to their children's hearing. Often, parents hear and remember certain information and discard other things. There is so much going on in the hearts of parents: learning how to cope, navigating family beliefs and perceptions of hearing loss, finding good supports, managing their children's behavior. Their hearts search for ways to help their children, as well as care for their families. They may need help releasing any emotional burden concealed in the heart in order to begin their learning journeys.

Helping parents become informed is a necessary step in their learning and development. Information feeds the mind and fuels the heart and can help parents relax in the face of inexperience. Information engages families and helps them make sense of their children's hearing loss. The more parents are informed, the more they make sense of their personal situations and their children's needs. Though the emotional and social contexts vary from family to family (parent experiences are directly linked to their pasts and cultures), parents need information that relates to and supports their personal circumstances.

When parents acquire information across the spectrum of hearing health and habilitation, they move closer to feelings of competence and empowerment. Knowledge helps parents become disciplined and engaged in a process to help their children. Knowledge helps parents make decisions and buy in to goals they seek for their children. When behaviors are directed at goals, it promotes a sense of purpose and gives parents personal satisfaction when achieved (Deci & Ryan, 2000). When parents participate in their children's progress, they continue to develop skills and grow through the experiences they have in helping their children succeed. Their progress is not measured by incentives or bribes, but by the degree of autonomy and competence they intrinsically feel.

## A Note to Practitioner

Further, parents have different personalities and they approach learning and parenting differently. Learning styles are generally grouped under four categories: "sensing," "intuitive," "feeling," and "thinking."[55] Observing the way parents learn can help practitioners put into perspective ways parents absorb and retain information. Researchers have also identified different approaches parents have to raising their children. *Authoritative* parents build relationships and rules. *Authoritarian* parents focus on obedience and discipline. *Permissive* parents don't enforce rules, while *uninvolved* parents provide little guidance.[56] While it's important not to categorize or label parents, personalities and learning styles among parents remain different and must factor into their behaviors and responses to how they learn and help their children's hearing loss and communication needs.

# Visualizing and Engaging in Goals

Parents need to visualize a clear path and future for their children. A future vision or goal becomes a bridge to journey onward. Perceptions often change over time, and the journeys parents face must include positive beliefs and embrace what is possible for their children. Helping children learn and grow, however, extends beyond parents' desires and dreams (or any perceptions they conjure); reaching any goal requires catching thoughts that deviate from the path and ensuring realistic steps are taken.

Some psychologists believe success and achievement is derived from the mind: how the mind habitually thinks rather than a skill set. The mind's divisive thoughts can lead to suffering and grief, especially when the mind ruminates in negativity, fixed mindset, or poor self-image. Thoughts can dictate the way people respond to the world, especially when not grounded in the present or in the truth. People need a sense of control in their lives. Learning to witness thoughts, through meditation or metacognition, is thought to impart greater control of the mind. When aware of what the mind is thinking, we can catch unrealistic assumptions and beliefs. We have a choice to shift the mind to something positive, such as an achievement or goal that promotes health and well-being.

Psychological growth also entails self-regulation of emotion, and a belief in the ability to succeed or accomplish a goal. It further requires optimism, dedication, and resilience. Getting to know ourselves and how we interrelate (in our communities, jobs, and families) asks us to also witness our emotional and experiential journeys, both positive and negative. Rather than getting caught in cycles of responsibilities, to-do lists, or emotional experiences, the getting-to-know the mind and the way we behave clears a path for self-determination and positive goal setting.

Regulating the mind is of value, and to get parents to buy in to a belief or a goal requires they participate in them with self-assurance and awareness. The mindfulness practice discussed earlier can help parents reflect on meaningful, productive steps to achieve any goal that fits their current situation. Through the practice, parents can ensure their thoughts are grounded in realism and that their decisions and goals are realistic and attainable.

Environments and cultures are often different for parents and must be taken into consideration. Some cultures embrace disabilities, other cultures banish them. Some parents are unable to walk down the street with their children. Others are willing to travel far distances for hearing tests, hearing devices, and parent support meetings. Parents intuitively respond to the needs of their children, and when they receive positive coaching and guidance that helps them visualize clear paths, they will move toward the actions and goals they can grasp.

Intrinsic and extrinsic motivation are highly influential factors of human behavior.[57] Parents need to realize their worth and believe they can succeed at decision making or, at best, help their children thrive. In the pursuit of goals parents embrace for their children, they need to feel self-assured. Feelings of worth and innate abilities to accomplish tasks and goals may need encouragement. Parents may act upon their children's communication and learning needs with more determination when they believe in themselves. As parents accomplish things successfully, they increase their confidence, interest in learning, and assurance in their actions. Goals can lead to action and actions can reinforce goals.

There are many examples of ways parents visualize and pursue goals to help their children succeed. Sacrifices are often made every day. Parents skip a day's pay to get support. A father and mother collect change from the community to pay for a bus ride ten hours from Haiti to the Dominican Republic to meet with audiologists on a service mission. A mother from Kenya travels with her two-year old son to a different country to receive a cochlear implant and auditory-based services. A family in India travels 36 hours once each month to receive auditory-verbal therapy. A mother creates her own signs and visual language, teaches them to her profoundly deaf son, and then tells her family to do the same for his benefit. Such parents demonstrate how powerful and engaging a parent can be! The passion of a parent cannot be underestimated, especially when they draw from intuition, face challenges with innate strengths, visualize a goal (or purpose), and believe in the ability to succeed.

> *Your beliefs become your thoughts,*
> *Your thoughts become your words,*
> *Your words become your actions,*
> *Your actions become your habits,*
> *Your habits become your values,*
> *Your values become your destiny.*
>
> *~ Mahatma Gandhi*

### A Note to Practitioner:

There is so much to be learned in the context of families and their children's hearing health needs and expectations. Humility can shape the way practitioners are empathetic to parents' unique personalities and circumstances. Fully attuning to and learning from parents means being compassionate and accepting of parents' perceptions and learning style. When parents share their insight, practitioners can follow the parents' thought processes and provide relational and informational supports that help parents see what is possible. As parents become informed about the needs of their children (such as communication development topics and hearing health care), practitioners can align lessons with parental capacity and the child's potential.

Practitioner priorities may be completely different from parents' views and interests. Meetings with parents are opportunities to learn as much about the family as possible and to provide relatable lessons in hearing health and communication. When parents are supported and their interests are embraced, they feel more empowered to participate in their children's development. A practitioner should guide the parent on a clear path of discovery and support parent's well-being. In other words, practitioners not only walk alongside parents to help them reach goals and higher expectations for their children, they must address parent emotions, beliefs, vision, purpose, and ways to cope.

## Summary

Positive psychology practices have evolved and grown throughout the world in recent decades. The impact varies across cultures; however, the science on positive psychology suggests benefits are universal. Undeniably, practitioners across the world regard mental health as essential for families who face disability and challenges related to the care given to their children. People respond differently to personal growth, and PGV argues that the activities presented in Part One enable caregiver empowerment and positive parenting journeys. Though intervention strategies have yet to be fully studied and measured among caregivers of children with hearing loss, PGV has witnessed immediate benefits of a positive psychology approach in workshops offered in India and Dominican Republic. Science indicates that developing presence of mind, cultivating gratitude, embracing self-compassion, being optimistic, and building resilience and personal insight foster well-being and pave the way for emotional and personal growth, which leads people to develop positive relationships with themselves, their children, and others who also support their children.[58]

PGV believes a positive psychology approach is the foundation to helping parents thrive and creating positive change in their lives and the lives of their children. The goal is to soften stigma, decrease feelings of shame, boost parent confidence, and cultivate positivity that foster parent empowerment. Parents must be emotionally equipped to cope with their journey as caregivers and advocates for their children. How they make sense of their lives and roles as caregivers of children with hearing loss is a predictor of how they parent, form relationships, or engage in their children's communication and learning. How well parents understand themselves can awaken deeper insight and open doors to their personal growth, emotional wellness, and ability to cope with hearing loss.

Practitioners can review and explore strategies that feel appropriate for the culture and family. While traveling to work or engaging with parents, think about which approach to foster well-being will serve your families best. Consider an approach to influence positive change. Start by implementing just one intervention, and then continue to explore the others. Each parent may embrace one practice over another, and it will be important to consider ones that engage parents most effectively. Strategies from Part One are summarized below.

- Parent Vision
- Transforming Limiting Beliefs
- Exploring Parent Emotions
- Positive Visualization
- Meaning and Purpose
- Mindfulness
- Meditation

- Introspection
- Self-Care and 5% More exercise
- Assessing Resilience
- Breathing Exercise
- Affirmations
- Practicing Gratitude
- Practicing Self-Compassion

Several themes that influence positive parent experiences are presented in an article published in the Journal of Deaf Studies and Deaf Education entitled *Hearing Parents' Appraisals of Parenting a Deaf or Hard of Hearing Child.* Although the study was not conducted in low resource communities, it does validate the vision practitioners must embrace across the world. Positive perceptions of hearing parents who raise children with hearing loss include "relishing the high moments, taking less for granted, appreciating everyday positives, increased involvement with the child, and feeling free to let go of worry and fear." Many practitioners and psychologists agree that parent interventions that improve parent perceptions are vital in helping parents increase positive experiences they have with their children and with their coping with hearing loss.

Amy Szarkowski and Patrick J Brice. "Hearing Parents' Appraisals of Parenting a Deaf or Hard of Hearing Child: Application of a Positive Psychology Framework," *Journal of Deaf Studies and Deaf Education*, (2016) 1-10.

# PART TWO

# Building Capacity: Personal Resources, Leadership, Character Strengths

# INTRODUCTION

Part Two of *Coaching and Empowering Caregivers of Children with Hearing Loss* presents two more domains of PGV's diagram on well-being: personal resources/leadership identification and character strengths. These domains become a source of inspiration for caregivers and gives them something practical to rely on. When mindset and energy shifts toward intrinsic qualities, caregivers see themselves with renewed potential. The application of personal resources, leadership conduct, and character strengths empower parents to respond and engage with greater self-assurance.

Identifying personal resources, leadership behaviors, and character strengths inspire and motivate caregivers to help their children in new ways. Positive aspects of their personalities are enlivened when parents learn to apply them. As a result, confidence and positive self-perceptions are enhanced, which not only contribute to the parent's efficacy but also to their ability to become key influencers of their children's communication and learning. Research indicates that self-understanding influences the way parents approach their role as caregivers of children. [59] The extent to which caregivers are openhearted and compassionate toward themselves can influence how responsive they are to the hearing health and habilitation needs of their children.

The domains presented in this section are especially important in low resource communities because many caregivers often lack self-esteem in their role as caregivers of children with hearing loss. Stigma, discrimination, and the absence of habilitation support can hinder a caregiver's full participation; thus, parents need something to boost their confidence, particularly in times of difficulty when they feel overwhelmed or dejected. Feeling good about oneself includes the reflection on character strengths and leadership styles, which lead to self-respect and positive parenting. Exploring resources, both external and personal, also gives parents something innately good to rely on and perhaps motivates parents to become their best.

Nurturing and caring for the hearing, communication, and learning needs of children with hearing loss is complex. Parent education involves knowledge in hearing health and habilitation as well as fostering parenting responsiveness. It also involves coaching or training that elicits parenting potential and the capacity to engage in the welfare of their children on a consistent basis. This necessitates attention be given to caregivers' personal resources, leadership behaviors, and character strengths.

# Parent Potential

*"Lineage, personality, and environment may shape you, but they do not define your full potential."* ~ Mollie Marti

Coaching and empowering parents involves nurturing their potential. Because parenting is an ongoing learning experience, knowledge of self can be the most precious gift and course of awakening. When parents explore, identify, and apply their natural abilities in parenting, they foster positive, empowering, and life enhancing experiences. Parents may need help becoming the parents they are capable of being. When positive self-perceptions bubble up from inside, parents engage in powerful ways to help their children succeed. When parents discover positive aspects of themselves, they often feel fulfilled in the care given to their children. The time they spend with their children, the bonds they create, and their determination to see their children succeed influence their children's progress and welfare. The more parents engage, the more they learn how they play an important role in their children's lives.

Simply being aware of positive qualities, parents feel more determined and confident. If parents believe in their capacity to parent and their innate potential, then they may rise above stigma and pursue what is possible for their children with confidence and intent. With perseverance, they may travel miles to visit a hearing clinic or find a school that will enroll their children. With love and kindness, they remain empathetic. With curiosity they may seek international missions and humanitarians to obtain hearing tests. They apply strengths of justice or hope when they make financial sacrifices to purchase Hearing Assistive Technologies (HAT) or habilitation services. The strengths parents have are expressed in their behaviors.

Parents want to care for their children. There are times when this is more difficult to do because of the many challenging situations parents encounter at home and in the community. External influences often get in the way (culture, beliefs, limited services, poverty). Parents need to understand that they have potential and psychological capital to draw upon in times of difficulty or possible doubt. Parent who discover and explore their potential inevitably foster their well-being and improve their quality of life.

Self-awareness exercises, such as "Your Best-Self," can help caregivers focus on qualities that elevate their self-esteem and positive self-perceptions. Jeffrey Huffman from Harvard Medical School states, "People who completed the Best Possible Self exercise daily for two weeks showed increases in positive emotions right after the two-week study ended. Those who kept up with the exercise even after the study was over continued to show increases in positive mood one month later."[60] The goal is for parents to discover positive attributes that make them feel good about themselves and which apply in their lives and with their children. Fostering parent potential involves understanding one's best-self.

## REFLECT ON YOUR BEST-SELF [61]

Take 15 minutes to walk through each step below. Complete "Your Best-Self" exercise and discover positive attributes that you offer the world.

1. Choose someone in your community that you admire most, someone with a personality and behavior you respect.
2. Think about the qualities of that person. Reflect on their actions, behaviors, and attitudes you like and appreciate.
3. List these qualities on paper.
4. Look at the list quickly and *circle* three qualities that inspire you most.
5. Do you see these three qualities in yourself?
6. When have you put forth these qualities?
7. Discuss your findings with someone else. Does this person see more good qualities in you than you do?

Parents need reminders that they have innate abilities to apply their best-self in parenting children with hearing loss. When they identify positive attributes in themselves, they feel encouraged and motivated to put forth their best-self with renewed enthusiasm.

Here are some questions practitioners can ask caregivers:

*What moments inspire you most when you are with your child?*

*In general, when do you notice your best-self being applied?*

*What qualities will help you overcome stigma or confront adversity?*

*What qualities do you use to engage in conversation and play with your child?*

*What qualities will help you accomplish a goal you set for your child?*

## A Note to Practitioner:

Practitioners are experts in their field and have many responsibilities. Their well-being matters just as much as the well-being of the families they serve. Thriving in any professional job requires practitioners recognize and apply their fullest potential while caring for self. Practitioners should consider an approach to their well-being that inspires them and awakens their abilities to successfully coach and empower caregivers.

*Coaching and Empowering Caregivers of Children with Hearing Loss* encourages practitioners to explore the domains of well-being and interventions that best support them emotionally and professionally. With the demands of work in low- and limited- resource environments, practitioners should consider an approach that boosts their enthusiasm and motivates them to endure the challenges they face in their jobs. They can explore their best-self! There may be opportunities to become forward thinking or optimistic about parent potential. Through a personal experience and application of strategies, practitioners may also discover which ones best influence positive change in caregivers they serve.

The identification and application of personal resources, leadership styles, and character discussed in this part may be most useful. When practitioners (and parents) mindfully apply intrinsic capital, innate strengths, and leadership potential to perform their jobs, their well-being improves and as a result, positive change may occur with the patients they serve.

The cultural context at work and with families are different. Having conversations with colleagues and reflecting on the following questions can help determine ways to best integrate domains of well-being from this section personally and professionally:

> *What motivates you to engage willingly and optimistically in the work you do?*
>
> *What leadership skills do you apply in life and at work?*
>
> *What strengths do you embrace? Which ones help you effectively communicate with others and the families you serve?*
>
> *In what context do you work and what resources do you have to help improve parent education? Are there people outside your organization that can help?*
>
> *Whom can you confide in about difficult parent/family cases or dilemmas you face?*
>
> *What current approaches have you used to improve the responsiveness of caregivers?*
>
> *With whom can you explore personal resources, leadership, and strengths practice?*

# PERSONAL RESOURCES

"The Greatest Achievement of the human spirit is to live up to one's opportunities and make the best of one's resources." ~ Luc De Clapiers

Parents want to see their children succeed socially, emotionally, academically, and cognitively. Unfortunately, some parents may find it difficult to support such success as they might be wrapped in grief and limiting supports. Their happiness might be smothered with a fear of not knowing anything about deafness or what the future entails. Economic hardship and negative disability attitudes coming from people in their community also make planning for their children's future worrisome. No parenting journey is easy, especially in low- and limited- resource environments where resources are scarce. To help parents cope and raise successful children, they need to draw upon all possible supports. Their journeys to raise their children with hearing loss demand parents find resources that support them.

There are basically two kinds of resource categories: personal and external. Parents do not necessarily understand or realize how valuable personal and external resources can be until they discover them. They typically rely on practitioners who are in the community or services that are visible in the community. Resources vary by country and community, and parents may need help to source what is available and supportive.

*Personal Resources:*

*Personal resources* are psychological capital, referred to as intrinsic factors such as optimism, self-efficacy, hope, and resilience. These resources influence attitude, perception, and behavior. [62] In positive psychology, psychological capital is a core construct for well-being and thriving. The availability of personal resources most influences parents' abilities to cope with their children's hearing loss.[63]

The awareness of intrinsic personality and potential can influence ways parents become motivated to nurture and help their children. Parents can ask themselves what drives them to be responsive to the needs of their children hearing. Assessing what is going on inside the heart and mind can help parents identify what feels inspiring and resourceful. They may discover innate qualities that drive the determination to help their children and enrich their lives. Intrinsic resources are essential in low resource communities, especially where parent supports are limited. With practitioner coaching, parents can explore psychological capital that is empowering. Instinct, mindset, positive social and emotional experiences, and spirituality are elements of personal capital that help parents engage and rise to their potential. Discovering personal resources can help parents cope with their journeys to care for their children. Children's learning and communication may depend on how well parents engage in their personal resources.

Further, when parents explore psychological capital, they rely on intuition, experience, and memory. The understanding of their emotions, self-regulation, resilience, and mindset can enable their success.

## *External Resources:*

*External resources* are tangible and relate to the physical environment, such as the home, the weather, money, and parent groups. External resources are such things as hospitals and educational institutions. Hearing health clinics and schools for the deaf might offer parent supports, workshops, and therapies. Social service organizations also offer counseling or programs to help parents attend to their needs as well as their children's health and education. Though training and expertise varies among organizations and communities, there is merit in exploring all available resource opportunities.

Further, praise given by practitioners and family members or success seen in adults with hearing loss also classify as external resources.

External resources serve and support parents and their children. This includes people to talk with about challenging situations or therapists that work in speech and hearing. Professionals have specialized skills and experiences, and they may help parents engage sensibly in resources they need. Parenting seminars, support groups, and aural/oral or sign language communication workshops are also examples of valuable external resources. When these resources are limited in the community, it may be necessary to investigate what is available outside the immediate environment. Parents may be willing to travel the distance to engage in these services and supports.

Practitioners can develop their own parent education and informational workshops. While these require financial as well as human resources, such programs are invaluable in the process of informing, supporting, and empowering parents. Workshops, parent support groups, and consultations help parents learn specific tasks, such as parenting with compassion, developing communication skills, or troubleshooting hearing devices.

There are also many available materials on the internet which can also be downloaded, printed, and given to parents. Practitioners can choose to create their own printed materials that inform parents. When developing materials, the reading level and topic should reflect parent interests and be culturally relevant. Content might relate to facts of hearing loss, communication choices, or bring to light limiting beliefs. Though posters, flyers, pamphlets, or "how to" guides can help families, these self-created and informational resources can also promote parent potential. They can also enhance the potential and successes of children who have hearing loss.

### A Note to Practitioner:

Practitioners want to educate and support parents; it's part of their job. Parents want information that prepares them for their role as caregivers. While it is essential to address a hearing health agenda and give parents information, it is equally important to help parents find resourceful supports to help them improve their quality of life and confidence as caregivers of children with hearing loss. Once parents access their available resources, especially personal, they develop self-assurance that can be invaluable and essential to their children's well-being.

Reflect on personal and external resources listed on the next page and ask parents to evaluate what inspires and supports them. This involves building parents' critical thinking skills. Parents need to learn how to think and act on their own. Practitioners can ask questions that get parents thinking about psychological capital and external resources. When parents see the range of their resources and experience how these help them with their children, parents feel immeasurably supported and can become forward thinking and empowered in further use of those resources.

# IDENTIFY YOUR PERSONAL & EXTERNAL RESOURCES

Help parents reflect on the resources listed on the chart below. Ask parents to consider or write how each category below supports or inspires them. While many people define personal and external resources differently, this exercise helps parents see they have more available resources than they might think.

| | |
|---|---|
| **State of Mind:** Recognize your outlook, attitude, expectations, and limitations. Are you optimistic? Pessimistic? Judgmental? Giving? Forgiving? Loving? Fearful? Worried? | |
| **Learning/Thinking:** Consider how you learn (Visual? Kinesthetic? Auditory?) What problem solving and decision-making skills might you have? For example, what would help you reach a goal or overcome a challenge? Are there decisions you often and easily make that you overlook because they are routine? Do your beliefs and values trigger those decisions? | |
| **Social Supports:** Identify parents, friends, professionals, family members, and community organizations that give you support. It could be a parent group, your church, a school, etc. Different social supports can also help you to become informed. Social supports can also embrace the emotional journey you may experience. | |
| **Emotional Support:** Reflect on whom you can talk with about your personal, emotional experiences. Other parents perhaps? Your practitioner? Beyond these resources, what might help you choose and control your emotional responses (ex. meditation, conversation with others, prayer, character strength of love, etc.)? | |
| **Role Models:** Who are the people in your life who inspire you, coach you, and/or give you an idea of what is possible among individuals with hearing loss? | |
| **Physical/Wellness:** How do you care for your mind and body? What exercise and self-care do you engage in? Are there things you want to do that you haven't had time for? | |
| **Spiritual:** How does faith (or your beliefs) influence how you approach life and your child? | |
| **Financial:** Reflect on your monetary situation in terms of money, barter, and other resources within your reach: hearing aid missions, food and clothing sources, school, parent education programs, community services. | |

Partners for A Greater Voice developed this chart using a variety of sources to help parents identify personal resources. A printable version may be found by visiting www.greatervoice.com/education modules, (2017).

# Thoughts on Leadership

Leaders are often seen as people who succeed in something, are optimistic, or have expertise in any one subject or vocation. However, the concept of leadership reaches further, and feelings regarding leadership varies greatly from one person to the next. Not everyone defines success or leadership the same way. People manage their lives with degrees of energy and initiative, and their leadership skills might be overlooked. There are people who take charismatic and passionate steps to reach a very personal, fulfilling goal, and other people who are cautious in their decision making and goal attainment. Some people persevere quietly to overcome fear of failure or to attain their vision of success. People possess different leadership qualities, often resembling ways they manage their life.

Ken Blanchard, renowned author and expert on management, presents four styles of leadership listed below. Blanchard states that there is no singular or best leadership style and, in general, approaches can blend. Consider how the following relates to the way you manage relationships, decisions, or your life:

**Directive:** Involves taking over a challenging situation and applying one's knowledge.

**Supporting:** Plays more of a motivational role.

**Coaching:** Supports the knowledge of others and helps them foster decisions and action themselves.

**Delegator:** Places more responsibility on the shoulders of others.

There are many different ways people manage a situation. Many styles and approaches to leadership involve personality and character. Review the styles of leadership and management on the next page to understand the diversity of behaviors people exhibit. Reflect on different situations that require different behaviors. What leadership characteristics within this list do you have? There can be more than one style you embrace or rely on.

### Leadership Styles

There are as many approaches to leadership as there are leaders, from Lewin's Leadership Styles framework of the 1930s to the more recent ideas about transformational leadership. There are also many general styles, including servant and transactional leadership.

Building awareness of leadership and management styles can help to define an approach that is effective.

# WHAT STYLES OF MANAGEMENT DO YOU RELATE TO?

Examine the list below that was published in the *Harvard Business Review* to identify styles of leadership and management (Karen West, 2015).[64] For practitioners, become aware of styles that help you learn about yourself as a leader parents look up to. You can determine which styles help you best coach and empower a parent. For parents, which ones do you relate to and feel most empowering? Learning when to use which style can help a person succeed in a wider variety of leadership contexts. Identifying styles of leadership and management can be empowering especially when applied.

*COLLABORATOR:* empathetic, team-building, talent-spotting, coaching oriented

*ENERGIZER:* charismatic, inspiring, connects emotionally, provides meaning

*PILOT:* strategic, visionary, adroit at managing complexity, open to input, team oriented

*PROVIDER:* action oriented, confident in own methodology, loyal to colleagues, driven to provide for others

*HARMONIZER:* reliable, quality-driven, execution-focused, creates positive and stable environments, inspires loyalty

*FORECASTER:* learning oriented, deeply knowledgeable, visionary, cautious in decision making

*PRODUCER:* task focused, results oriented, linear thinker, loyal to tradition

*COMPOSER:* independent, creative, problem solving, decisive, self-reliant

## A Note to Practitioner:

Practitioners may want to identify and explore how these leadership and management styles apply at work and in their practice. They can notice when they are a *collaborator* or a *problem solver*, or when they are an *energizer* or a *provider* while working with parents. Practitioners can also talk with parents about their behaviors and help parents recognize and reflect on management styles to which they feel most connected. Parent input is important. Parents may choose several styles of management to fit the perceptions of themselves. People need not be limited to a single style; it is possible to have more than one style to rely on.

Practitioners boost parent morale when they encourage or praise parents for their application of management and leadership conduct. When parents realize how their actions influence their children's development or their ability to become effective leaders, they deepen their understanding of themselves. How they respond to their children's hearing loss and become empowered might be fostered when they view themselves as leaders. Referring to leadership styles on page 91 (*Assessment: What's Your Management Style?*, HBR 2015), here are examples:

- When parents are **collaborative** in nature, they seek to teach others about their children's hearing loss, assistive technologies, and needs for inclusion.
- Parents who show interest in learning and want to share their insights and ideas with practitioners exhibit the management style of a **forecaster**.
- Being decisive and wanting to find solutions can mean a parent is a **composer**.
- When parents monitor their children closely, provide consistent discipline, and express control they are **authoritative**. These parents are supportive and encouraging. They are often resilient.[65]

Parents can create positive change in their children's education and hearing health services when they apply leadership and management behaviors directed at their children's needs. For example, a father in the Dominican Republic explains to a group of parents how he pays for his son's cochlear implant surgery and device. He describes how customs officers try to charge him exorbitant taxes on the importation of replacement parts. Though he worries about broken parts and a failing telecoil, he learns about the disability laws in his country and finds a section that implies that no tariff will be made on medical devices for persons with disabilities. He uses good judgement, emotional regulation, and perseverance to travel a long distance and show customs officers this section of the disability law. He demonstrates the management styles of a *composer* and a *provider*. Parents can become strong advocates for the rights and needs of their children when they draw upon intrinsic qualities.

# LEADERSHIP AND TRUST

Effective leadership is built on trust. How do practitioners instill trust and how do families see them as leaders? Reflect on the categories below and determine how well you demonstrate these behaviors when working with caregivers. Remain consistent in demonstrating the following behaviors on a regular basis to build and maintain trust.

## Vision

Believe in something bigger than today. Be willing to share this with parents and engage them in goals you seek. Keep your focus on the present needs of parents, but always think ahead toward how you can grow, improve, and learn with participating families.

## Authenticity

Be yourself all the time. Parents will come to know you and what to expect from you. Be willing to share something about yourself and know it's okay to be vulnerable. Parents want to hear your stories, successes, and challenges, so be honest about your experiences. Being truthful and comfortable with "you" will help you to connect and build trust.

## Commitment

Remain dedicated to your causes: family education, community outreach, parent group networks. Remain faithful as you work through your processes, projects, and programs. Communicate your dedication and demonstrate it in your actions, which will help everyone to stay in alignment with your overall purpose and mission.

## Transparency

Share information on what you know, ways to take action, and the reason why you made a decision. If you don't do this, people will come to their own conclusions. Keep other practitioners and interested parents in the loop. Keep parents informed, even if you have to tell them "I don't know but will let you know when I have more information."

## People

You need others to help you achieve your goals. Recognize them, provide feedback, and guide them to be successful. Some people might be able to help you build parent supports. Be approachable and open to their concerns. They will learn to trust that you value them and are there for them.

## Character

Great leaders have integrity, high morals, and qualities others want to adopt. Be the person others want to be. Your strong character traits will help inspire others to follow your lead and to align their actions with the goals you seek for their children.[66]

Virginia Maglio, Learning and Development Consultant, created for PGV, (2017).

# Emotional Intelligence, a Leadership Asset

Leadership skills are broad reaching. They include qualities such as good listening, independence, empathy, sound decision making, creativity, charisma, and reliability.[67] Though knowledge of a subject matter is important (such as audiology, auditory development, sign language, or social work), expertise isn't the only sign of an effective leader. Daniel Goleman in his book *Emotional Intelligence (EI)* states that "abilities rather than IQ or technical skills emerge as the "discriminating" competency that best predicts who among a group of very smart people will lead most ably."[68] Thus, what Goleman found and recent research supports is that while intelligence or technical skills are important aspects to leadership, emotional intelligence is also an asset.

**What makes up emotional intelligence?** Goleman identifies a key set of Emotional Intelligence characteristics. They include the abilities to motivate oneself and persist through frustrations, to control impulses, to regulate one's moods and not let distress impact the ability to think, to empathize, and to hope.[69] While these human aspects of leadership are not the elements we most quickly acknowledge, the research clearly identifies them as critical to effective leadership.

Emotional Intelligence (EI) evolves throughout a lifetime, and it is an invaluable set of abilities and traits. Leaders must learn to trust and build relationships that are mutually beneficial, and their EI can support this.

## A Note to Practitioner:

EI is important in the relationship the practitioner develops with a parent, especially when considering the parents' emotional journey. Empathy is needed to understand the parent context, to be sensitive to parent experiences, and to comprehend challenges the parent endures. Parents have different needs than their children; thus, attuning empathetically to the interests, feelings, and thoughts of parents is a skill. Practitioners who develop emotional intelligence encourage an ability to be open-minded and supportive of the parent perspective; they also draw parents closer.

Equally, emotional intelligence can help parents connect to their feelings, manage their stress, turn intention into action, and make informed decisions about the things that matter most. As stated before, EI is an ability to motivate oneself and persist through frustrations, to control impulses, and to hope - all critical to effective leadership. Parents must first be cognizant of their thoughts and behaviors before they understand or evaluate why they respond or react in a certain way (refer to coping strategies in Part One). When parents are aware of their reactions and emotional responses, they see reasons for their behaviors more clearly. With reflection, parents may discover what motivates them to manage their children's needs and make decisions. This presents opportunities for parents to find what is truthful and intrinsically empowering.

Practitioners can support parents' growth in many ways, and just by talking about EI parents may progress in such areas as self-regulation, perspective, forgiveness, and judgement (critical thinking). Strong EI might help parents engage in better decision making, goal directed behavior, and optimism.[70] While a variety of skills are needed to support the development of children's communication, socio-emotional growth, and cognition, EI remains fundamental to the application of these skills and behaviors that engage parents.

EI is important to leadership growth and an assessment can provide insight to coaching and parent support practices. Complete the exercise on the next page to assess your emotional intelligence.

> Peter Salovey and John Meyers wrote: "EI is the ability to perceive emotions, to access and generate emotions so as to assist thought, to understand emotions and emotional knowledge, and to reflectively regulate elements so as to promote emotional and intellectual growth."

# EMOTIONAL INTELLIGENCE ASSESSMENT TOOL[71]

| EI Component | EI Ratings | | | |
|---|---|---|---|---|
| **Intrapersonal** | Never | Sometimes | Frequently | Always |
| Self-awareness: See self as talented and capable of meeting challenges. | | | | |
| Self-regulation: Able to control emotions and impulses and redirect to fulfill obligations. | | | | |
| Flexibility: Open to new experiences and application. | | | | |
| Motivation: Pursue goals with energy and optimism. | | | | |
| Achievement: Demonstrate drive to do well within defined structure. | | | | |
| Initiative: Recognize when to take independent action | | | | |
| Resilience: Remain encouraged and persistent when things don't go as planned. | | | | |
| Well-being: Maintain good physical and mental condition and access available coping resources. | | | | |
| **Interpersonal** | Never | Sometimes | Frequently | Always |
| Demonstrative empathy: Sensitive to others' needs and able to comfort. | | | | |
| Energy: Commitment toward others by doing and acting. | | | | |
| Social skill: Proficient and comfortable building and maintaining relationships. | | | | |
| Tolerance: Patient and respectful during disagreements and conflict with others. | | | | |
| Persuasiveness: Effectively share ideas and solicit those of others. | | | | |
| Ability to lead: Develop staff by influencing them to challenge themselves and supporting them in goal achievement. | | | | |

Adapted from *Introduction to Type and Emotional Intelligence* by Roger R. Pearman.

# Fostering Parent Leaders

People often view leaders as those who reach success in their job or status in life. Leaders are sources of inspiration and can bestow their professional skills and invaluable knowledge on others. Practitioners often assume leadership roles because of their expertise. Parents need guidance from them. They often view doctors, audiologists, teachers of the deaf, or speech therapists as leaders and rely on them for information and their children's specialized care. Practitioners might be the only person parents can talk with, and thus caregivers often trust in their experience.

Parents of children with hearing loss might not know they have leadership potential, such as the ability to communicate well, to bring people together, to motivate and inspire, and to trust and build trust. Coaching parents must include ways to foster their self-knowledge as well as their ability to manage and lead their children through stages of their development. When leadership and management skills become known, parents may engage in hearing health, become forward thinking, and solve problems themselves.

> "There are hundreds of parents who have spearheaded their children's education and success. I admire their perseverance, integrity, unconditional love, and zest for wanting the best for their children. These parents are inspirational, and they emerge as strong leaders of their children's development. They become role models for others" (J. Travers).

Good leaders are patient listeners (parents learn to watch the behavior of their children and attune to their needs). Good leaders let others act on innovations that can drive a mission or cause forward (parents choose creative ways to engage with their children). Good leaders have empathy (parents listen to their children and respond to the needs of the children with more self-compassion).

Even in challenging situations and when confronting community stigma, parents persevere. As parents become more conscious and understanding of their personality and innate qualities, they are often inspired by their competencies and skills. As a result, they may expand their level of engagement and management of their children's needs with greater determination. They respond to their children's needs or themselves more favorably when they experience a sense of accomplishment.

Further, many parents become specialists. Their learning evolves and they become proficient in hearing aid care, child advocacy, or social networking. Some parents pursue and obtain certification in audiology and hearing and speech. Others will demonstrate competency and assurance, which can be a source of inspiration and support to other parents in the community. Parents who provide support to other parents are also leaders. Even without professional training, a supportive parent is a good role model and an important personal and external resource. Given the fact that hearing and language development are imperative for children with hearing loss, low- and limited- resource environments may very well need parents to become specialists.

## Character Strengths

"I do not believe you should devote much effort to correct your weakness. Rather, I believe the highest success in living and the highest emotional satisfaction comes from building and using our signature strengths." ~ Dr. Martin Seligman

Our environment often predicts or supports how our skills and talents are nurtured, and every person has an opportunity to develop themselves through experience and practice. We can be surrounded by musicians and learn how to sing, dance, chant, or play an instrument. We can live among laborers and learn a vocation and trade. Our fathers, mothers, aunts, and uncles teach us many skills. Our environment often predicts how we make use of our talents in life.

Beyond our environment, each of us is born with a personality mapped into our brains, cells, and tissues. From our ancestors we acquire genetic traits that are embedded in the brain and marked by DNA. There is the belief that DNA also contains things like temper and disposition.[72] Our education, culture, and relatives are also factors contributing to personality. The essence of personality unfolds over a lifetime, and through experience people learn certain things and develop many skills. They can also learn about themselves, their capabilities, and strengths through their experiences and interactions with others.

Psychologist Martin Seligman suggests becoming aware of and building upon twenty-four innate character strengths. Skills and talents can be refined, and while strengths are embedded in personality, they can also be cultivated. The 24-character strengths are nested within six virtue categories: Wisdom, Temperance, Justice, Humanity, Courage, Transcendence. The character strengths are pathways to the virtues. Our environment or situation often predicts how character strengths emerge or how they are exercised. When people focus on character strengths, they cultivate these internal capacities. Rather than dwelling on limitations, Seligman sees a character strengths approach as a way to foster positive psychological well-being.[73]

## *What are VIA Character Strengths?*

Philosophers and scientists have long studied positive psychology. In the early 2000s, however, Seligman and a team of scientists studied innate human characteristics across the world and in different cultures. They wanted to find a common thread among the human race. A three-year project involving 55 distinguished scientists devoted to evaluating character traits resulted in a classification of virtues and character strengths, and a discovery and investigation of positive traits in human beings (Peterson & Seligman, 2004). Seligman and Peterson identified twenty-four strengths found in all human beings and categorized these under six virtues. These character strengths are found to be universal across cultures and religions. VIA Classification of character offers science a way to explore how people engage in life, including goals they seek, plans they make, and relationships they develop.[74] Since 2000, hundreds of peer-reviewed articles have been published across many cultures regarding character strengths.

Dr. Ryan Niemiec describes character strengths in his book *Mindfulness and Character Strengths*. The word "character" conjures up a number of meanings for people, such as one's reputation, one's principles or ideologies, or one's values such as wisdom, honesty, or integrity. People tend to think of character as something permanent and unchanging. The actual meaning of the word "character" refers to qualities that are distinctive to an individual. Because there is a unique blend of 24-character strengths innate in all humans, being aware of and knowing how to apply any singular or combination of strengths will contribute to a person's ability to flourish. Throughout a person's life, these strengths can be explored.

People's strengths are expressed in a variety of ways, and character traits often overlap in any given situation. Strengths are relational and are often linked; one strength is not necessarily isolated from another. No two people express their strengths in the same way, and any combination of strengths may be present in any given situation. Typically, there are a few strengths that more easily and naturally surface on a regular basis, but all strengths appear in a person's life. Personalities, which are generally stable, develop over time - as do character strengths throughout a person's life.

The classification of character strengths has been studied across cultures, and the words chosen to categorize these strengths may vary to some degree in some countries. Different words or phrases to describe a person's positive traits and aspects of personality would likely fall into one of the six virtues seen in the table below. Local dialects and cultures may have similar ways to describe the essence and meaning of individual strengths, which are grouped together in the VIA Institute's Classification of Virtues and Associated Character Strengths shown on the next page.

# VIA Institute's Classification of Six Virtues and 24 associated Character Strengths:

| WISDOM | COURAGE | HUMANITY |
|---|---|---|
| Creativity | Bravery | Love |
| Curiosity | Perseverance | Kindness |
| Judgment | Honesty | Social Intelligence |
| Love of Learning | Zest | |
| Perspective | | |

| JUSTICE | TEMPERANCE | TRANSCENDENCE |
|---|---|---|
| Teamwork | Forgiveness | Appreciation of Beauty & Excellence |
| Fairness | Humility | Gratitude |
| Leadership | Prudence | Hope |
| | Self-Regulation | Humor |
| | | Spirituality |

### *Why do character strengths matter to caregivers of children with hearing loss?*

Potential awaits inside everyone. Strengths are part of humanity, and when applied can enhance self-esteem, increase vital involvement, and augment achievement. In many ways, strengths awareness and the practice of using strengths can help parents achieve many things in life with optimism. When parents lead with character strengths in mind, they engage in positive ways to approach life's challenges and build meaningful relations.

Ryan Niemiec, one of the leading practitioners of character strengths today, suggests that simply being mindful of one's strengths has many benefits and understanding character strengths can have a significant and positive impact on one's life. Research in positive psychology shows that becoming aware of and using character strengths can help us:

- Buffer against, manage, and overcome problems,
- Improve our relationships,
- Enhance health and overall well-being.[75]

Character strengths are innate and are seen in people across cultures. A focus on character strengths can help parents in developing countries to become aware of their virtues, and which can build their self-confidence. This emerging awareness shifts attention away from feelings of grief, stigma and worry. Parents feel a greater sense of worthiness when courage, humanity, or wisdom are employed, and these character strengths become a tool for cheerfulness and self-efficacy. Examples include *courage* to ask for help and express feelings, *love* to respond to the child's needs, *perseverance* to achieve a goal, *curiosity* to learn about communication opportunities, and *perspective* to remain even tempered. Parents who become aware of their strengths and mindfully focus on them will open more doors to positive behaviors and outlook.

In his book *Mindfulness and Character Strengths*, Ryan Niemiec examines mindfulness and practical use of character strengths. He suggests four simple ways to approach character strengths intervention. The process is discussed next and includes how to identify, explore, apply, and reflect on strengths.

# How to Coach using Character Strengths

There are many ways to learn about strengths and to incorporate them into hearing health practices and the lives of caregivers. Coaching caregivers to use their strengths is a process that requires multiple visits. It is useful to notice and appreciate how parents' top strengths naturally emerge. All strengths can be developed and utilized across different situations.

The first step is to find opportunities that allow parents to safely identify their top strengths and explore those they relate to most easily. The process begins with the identification of just one strength. Parents may need help recognizing their most natural strength that helps with their approach to engaging in life and their children's development. Then, other strengths can be explored and applied.

The VIA Strengths Survey is a scientific tool that quickly helps caregivers identify their top strengths. It is offered on the internet for free and is available in dozens of languages. An office computer may be necessary to help parents access this online survey, and practitioners can help parents read survey questions if necessary. Once completed, an easy-to-read report is generated at no extra cost (http://www.viacharacter.org). It is recommended to first choose only 2 or 3 top strengths and reflect and practice using them.

Good opportunities to discuss and explore character strengths often occur during parent group meetings, workshops, and individual hearing and speech therapy sessions. During these events, virtues and individual character strengths are illuminated through parents' storytelling and narratives which often illustrates their positive traits.

## *Identifying and Spotting Strengths in Parents*

Spotting strengths in parents can occur the moment parents walk into the room. The way they walk, speak, and communicate with practitioners about the needs of their children in situations in their home environment are opportunities to learn something about parents' personalities and behaviors. Many parents are quiet and wait for practitioners to lead; others may sit on the edge of their seat trying to learn more ways to support their children's hearing and progress. Nonverbal and verbal cues can be clues to spotting character strengths. The ways in which parents behave around their children can reveal character traits. Strengths of love, kindness, perseverance, or curiosity are common. A practitioner can say," I see how much you love your child" or "I notice how you are very curious about technology." "I hear how you are determined to find a school for your child." They can also encourage parents to identify strengths seen in themselves as well.

Since strengths typically occur in constellations, more than one strength can be observed in parenting scenarios. The first step is identifying naturally occurring strengths in combinations and then specifying the positive consequence of using that strength. It is most useful when identifying strengths to point out behaviors that demonstrate strengths. For example, "I noticed how you bent down to talk with your child face-to-face. Your compassion and perspective in kindly getting down on their level helps them feel valued and shows that you care that they understand."

Spotting dominant strengths in parents during appointments is an important opportunity to share any positive trait that emerges, especially when parents explain how they interact with their children at home. Practitioners can talk with parents about the character strengths they spot and then challenge parents to notice their own strengths as they go about their day at work and at home with their children.

## *Exploring Character Strengths*

Self-awareness of all prevailing character strengths is important for parents to grasp. Good opportunities to delve into strengths exploration can be during parent meetings and workshops. Strengths should be explicitly explained and presented. The narratives parents share contain examples. When parents disclose stories about their own family situation, a facilitator can point out character strengths to the group at large. This may help other parents see character traits in themselves. The exploration of strengths is very effective when parents learn about them with peers in the same room. Peer support permits parents to express themselves freely and securely among people who share similar experiences. It is not threatening to explore strengths and learn how they influence parental attitudes and responsiveness to their children's development and needs.

The most common character strengths are kindness, fairness, judgement, curiosity, and honesty.[76] Typically, parents go about their day unaware of the strengths they use. As parents respond to questions and share personal stories, practitioners can spot strengths that naturally arise and elicit feelings of cheerfulness or delight. Parents may need help to discover commonly applied strengths. Should parents more easily identify with talents and skills (such as cooking, dancing, or driving a motorcycle), then practitioners can help parents explore one or two character strengths that align with these. It is important to point out how parents may already be applying common strengths in the nurturing care they give to their families.

## *Applying Strengths*

Once strengths are identified and explored, practitioners can encourage ways parents apply strengths. Balancing instructions on hearing health care and communication development with mindful discussion of parents' character strengths can be an effective way to encourage caregivers' participation. Every opportunity to enhance the relationship between parent and child in meaningful ways contributes to the children's development, and the understanding and application of character strengths facilitates more meaningful engagement. Parental empowerment is enhanced when parents apply innate capabilities naturally and see themselves as important contributors.

A strength of curiosity, for example, can help parents see the world as a playground for their children. With fairness, parents respond to their children's unique needs and ensure their children get supports that help them hear and learn. Kindness is expressed when parents do good deeds for others and are self-compassionate. Self-regulation helps parents cope with community stigma and build resilience. When parents present themselves in authentic and genuine ways, they exhibit honesty. And with creativity, parents search for fun ways to spend time with their children while expanding their world of learning.

A mother lived alone with her daughter in a poor section of San Andres, cast out of her own family's house when her daughter was diagnosed as deaf. PGV consulted with her about the Hearing Assistive Technologies, and more importantly reminded her of her strengths of love and humility. We explained how her strengths deepen her bond with her daughter and how she could develop her child's listening and speaking skills in the quiet of her own space. There were no distractions that prevented this mother from engaging with her child. And beyond the comfort of her home, she traveled with her daughter by bus to the city every weekday to an oral school. With strengths of resilience and zest, she found a modest, part-time job during school hours and sometimes volunteered in her daughter's classroom. With good judgement and kindness, she spent nearly every waking hour with her daughter outside work and school. Her child was happy and learning and thriving because of her mother's unconditional love.

Strengths can be spotted, explored, and applied in many different ways. Here are some examples of how parents apply their strengths:

- A strength of Perseverance can help parents ensure their children wear their hearing devices throughout the day and learn to listen.

- A strength of Love and Kindness can help parents to discipline their children.

- A strength of Prudence and Curiosity can motivate parents to attend meetings.

- A strength of Perspective and Love of Learning can help parents remain open minded to meeting new people and learning from others.

- A strength of Creativity and Curiosity can support a parent's ability to find external resources and explore ways to nurture their children's language.

- An Appreciation of Beauty and Curiosity can facilitate ways parents engage in talking with their children in new and playful ways.

## *Applying Strengths in Difficult Situations*

Practitioners can also encourage caregivers to apply their best qualities during moments of despair and challenge. A character strengths approach helps parents manage problems and improve relationships. The goal is to influence positive mentality around parenting abilities, and to engage parents in productive, healthy behaviors and relationships that ultimately support their children. When a strengths-based approach is practiced, it helps parents shift thoughts away from potentially negative self-perceptions or worry to the possibilities of their children reaching their potential. To encourage and motivate parents to persevere at home and in their relationships, reassure parents of one or two leading strengths and reiterate the ways parents have already applied their strengths naturally.

> Research shows that *actively* and *deliberately* infusing your character strengths into your daily life can lead to greater well-being, stronger relationships, increased engagement at work, and more happiness (VIA Institute on Character, 2018).

By focusing on the foremost qualities of parents, practitioners can help parents overcome difficult situations and experience how their goodness contributes to their well-being as well as their children's progress. Character strengths practice is a powerful tool that helps parents set goals, make decisions, problem solve, and parent successfully. It can be applied in any situation. Challenging situations are often opportunities to put strengths into action, for example:

- When parents discipline children, suggest they turn to the strength of kindness or fairness.

- When parents find it hard to communicate about their needs or the needs of their children, have them turn to their strength of courage, zest, love, or teamwork.

- When parents are overcome with fear or worry, ask them to recall strengths of forgiveness, honesty, or self-regulation.

## *Helping Caregivers Apply Strengths with their Children*

Caregivers of children with hearing loss in low- and limited- resource environments can be the primary mentors of their children's success. Children's social and emotional development are often dependent upon the nurturing and learning they receive from parents and others who care for them. Often, parents need encouragement to interact with their children, to talk with their children's school or to help their children expand their learning. A character strengths approach helps parents build parental capacity to nurture and support children.

Practitioners can ask parents the following questions:

> *What do you feel when you notice that strength in yourself?*
>
> *What other strengths are you aware of when you engage with your child or spouse?*
>
> *How might you practice a strength when helping your child communicate and learn?*
>
> *How might you practice that strength when you need to discuss your child's needs?*
>
> *How can you use your character strengths to build relationships?*

The awareness and application of strengths helps improve parent-child interactions, build healthy relationships, foster better communication, and enhance overall well-being. For example, parents' strength of love and kindness can be applied when communicating and playing with their children. Parents will discover how their children learn new words and complex sentences when they use a strength of zest or humor to promote language. Parents boost overall feelings of positivity when they learn how strengths help them communicate more confidently with families and schools. Even with difficult conversations, parents will experience how empowering it can be when they apply their strengths to advocate for their children's education and needs.

Recall how positive psychology suggests focusing on what works, what is good, and what can influence a positive mindset. What matters most is parents' self-perceptions of their abilities to parent, regardless of their perception of hearing loss. Interventions that infuse character strengths invoke parents' confidence, and they may act with more love, courage, and self-assurance. Mindful awareness and use of innate character strengths can also foster parents' motivation to address their children's learning needs. Strengths energize and inspire new ways parents can respond to their children's communicative, learning, and developmental needs. Parents may participate in hearing health and habilitation in more constructive ways when they actively engage in strengths practice.

## A Note to Practitioner:

You might find character strengths coaching more beneficial once you personally experience and explore your dominant strengths. Take the online VIA survey to identify your top strengths, and then explore and apply two or three top strengths at work and with the families you serve. When you go about your day, notice when these strengths appear and expand your awareness of strengths you apply naturally. When you coach and counsel parents, engage in strengths that are natural for you and ones which you connect with effortlessly. Notice when strengths help you to improve relationships, buffer against stress, and make good decisions. Do you feel energized or more engaged in the work you perform?

You can move from personal experience of character strengths exploration and practice to character strengths interventions with the parents you serve. First identify two or three key strengths in a parent, and then help parents become aware of them. Give parents time to process and understand their strengths. Discuss how strengths can help them cope better, build relationships, and/or safeguard against grief.

With practice, parents can influence their children's progress using their strengths as their guide. As parents get more comfortable leading with strengths, they begin to recognize and reinforce their own strengths. Parents need significant exposure to understand and cultivate character strengths, and when parents receive coaching to use their strengths in the nurturing care given to their children, their children profit. There is a trickle-down effect when strengths are tapped.

**Practitioner Strengths and Well-being**

**Parent Strengths and Well-being**

**Child Strengths and Well-being**

# CHARACTER STRENGTHS ASSOCIATIONS

**Noted in Peterson and Seligman (2004):** Used with approval. Copyrighted by Ryan M. Niemiec, Mindfulness and Character Strengths, A Practical Guide to Flourishing, pgs. 35-36, Hogrefe Publishing, 2014.

*Creativity:* Open to new experiences; cognitive flexibility.

*Curiosity:* Desire for challenge in work or play; goal oriented; adept at making complex decisions; willingness to challenge stereotypes; sense of subjective well-being.

*Judgement:* Adept at problem solving; cognitive ability; effective in dealing with stress; more resistant to suggestions and manipulation.

*Love of Learning:* More adept at navigating challenges; more likely to seek/accept challenges; autonomy; resourcefulness; self-efficacy; healthy; less stressed.

*Perspective:* Life satisfaction; even tempered; social intelligence; maturity; open-mindedness; sociability; social intelligence; successful aging.

*Bravery:* Prosocial oriented; internal locus of control; self-efficacy; ability to delay gratification; tolerance for uncertainty; capacity to assess risk; capacity for reflection; capacity to create and sustain high quality connections with others.

*Perseverance:* Achievement/goal completion; resourcefulness; self-efficacy.

*Honesty:* Positive mood; life satisfaction; openness to new experience; empathy; conscientiousness; effort; capacity for self-actualization; emotional stability.

*Zest:* Autonomy; connection with others; goal attainment

*Love:* Positive relationship with others; positive social functioning; higher self-esteem; capacity to cope with stress; healthy balance between dependency and autonomy.

*Kindness:* Overall mental and physical health; longevity.

*Social Intelligence:* Smooth social functioning; life judgements; lower levels of aggression.

# CHARACTER STRENGTHS ASSOCIATIONS

**Noted in Peterson and Seligman (2004):** Used with approval. Copyrighted by Ryan M. Niemiec, Mindfulness and Character Strengths, A Practical Guide to Flourishing, pgs. 35-36, Hogrefe Publishing, 2014.

*Teamwork:* Social trust; positive view of human nature.

*Fairness:* Perspective; self-reflection; cooperation; leadership; prosocial behavior.

*Appreciation of Beauty:* Openness to experience; capacity for change/self-improvement; altruism; devotion to others/larger community.

*Leadership:* Cognitive skills/intelligence; flexibility/adaptability; emotional stability; integrity; interpersonal skills; creativity/resourcefulness; internal locus of control.

*Spirituality:* Positive social relationships; forgiveness; kindness; compassion; sense of purpose; happiness; capacity to cope with illness and stress; self-regulation.

*Forgiveness:* Prosocial behaviors; agreeableness; lower levels of anger, anxiety, and hostility; emotional stability.

*Gratitude:* Positive emotions; optimism; longevity; life satisfaction; openness to experience; conscientiousness; lower levels of anxiety; improved immunity.

*Humility:* Perspective; forgiveness; capacity to attain self-improvement goals; self-regulation.

*Hope:* Achievement; positive relationships; physical well-being; active problem solving; conscientiousness; diligence.

*Prudence:* Cooperative; interpersonal warmth; assertiveness; curiosity, insightfulness; optimism; imaginative; high achievement/performance.

*Humor:* Positive mood; capacity to manage stress; creativity; intelligence; less neuroticism.

*Self-Regulation:* High levels of academic achievement; self-esteem; self-acceptance; capacity to control anger; perceived by others as more likeable/trustworthy.

> **EXERCISE YOUR CHARACTER STRENGTHS:**
>
> 1. Identify your top two or three character strengths.
> 2. Identify your top three or five leadership/management styles.
> 3. Identify your top three or five personal resources.
> 4. What is the relationship between your character strengths and the leadership/management styles you circled in the previous section?
> 5. What is the relationship between your character strengths and personal resources?

### A Note to Practitioner:

*Coaching and Empowering Caregivers of Children with Hearing Loss, an approach to foster well-being* does not include a complete course on character strengths intervention. Workshops with trained professionals in the practice will help to deepen knowledge, experiences, and practice. Training can specifically target the most effective interventions for supporting parents' culture, community, and family. Refer to resources in the back of this book or reach out to PGV for further information.

## Summary

Managing and caring for a child's hearing and development is a journey filled with a matrix of emotions, knowledge, behaviors, skills development, and personal growth. The resilience parents develop carries them forward, yet parents must be equipped to make decisions and act on goals they want for their children. A reflection and application of strengths, leadership styles, and personal resources can support caregivers' self-sufficiency and belief in their successful journeys. Intrinsic qualities, such as natural leadership and character strengths, influence a person's actions and conduct. When parents embrace these aspects of their personality and behavior, they develop personal power, an ability to influence positive change and outcomes, and their sense of self-determination in the care given to their children. An empowered parent is resourceful.

# PART THREE

## COACHING CAREGIVERS:
### PARENT SUPPORTS

# Introduction

The domains of well-being presented in Parts One and Two play a vital role in successful parenting journeys. Optimism, growth mindset, resilience, coping strategies, personal resources, leadership styles, and character strengths are approaches that foster parental capacity and efficacy, and which empower parents in unique ways. Part Three describes parents supports, coaching and empowering, empathetic listening, communication opportunities, relationships, and ways to start parent groups. Parent supports and successful coaching can strengthen parental responsiveness to hearing health practices and effectively engage them in their children's learning and communication development.

When mentored and guided with appropriate, timely, and relatable supports, parents engage in a course of action relevant to their needs and the needs of their children. Parents need to form relationships that help them grow in confidence and competence, which are important to their well-being. According to psychologists Edward Deci and Richard Ryan, there are three fundamental and universal needs that are essential for psychological health and motivation. These needs include developing competence (knowledge and skills), autonomy (independence), and psychological relatedness (compassion).[77] They influence how people act, behave, and engage.

Parents behave differently, and they cope with a variety of challenges in low- and limited- resource communities. Practitioners must fully understand parents and their family context, culture, and beliefs. Meaningful parent engagement and empowerment in hearing health and habilitation practices involves creating, fostering, and strengthening parent supports that help them cope.

Especially in low- and limited- resource communities, many parents are accustomed to receiving practitioner direction and recommendations. Practitioners assume many responsibilities and they cannot possibly be there to guide parents every step of the way. Though parents often listen and wait for step-by-step instructions, they eventually need to feel empowered to help their children at any stage of their development. Supporting parents must ultimately enable parent potential and foster a pathway toward **self-determination.**

> Self-determination in psychology refers to both intrinsic, human motivation to make decisions and people's tendencies and innate personality to learn and grow (en.m.wikipedia.org). Basic human needs for autonomy, competence, and relatedness foster self-determination (Deci & Ryan, 2008).

# Parent Supports

Parent supports are any service provided to parents that helps them learn, access resources, cope, and make decisions that support their children's development. Supports often demand practitioners with specialized skills and training: audiology, aural/oral habilitation, sign language instruction, social services, psychology.

Practitioners often assess what is a priority for parents of children with hearing loss, and they help parents navigate hearing health and habilitation services that are available in their communities. The challenge in many low-and limited- resource communities is also finding professional services, coaching, and parent supports. Children may have different developmental needs, and related supports may require professionals outside hearing health to address the unique needs of both parents and their children.

David Luterman, a professor emeritus of Communication Disorders at Emerson College in Boston, Massachusetts, who has supported parents since the 1960s, suggests counseling needs to shift to parents' learning and growth. Luterman defines parent supports as those needed to embrace emotions and coping as priorities for progress.[78] A child's ability to communicate is critical, yet rather than getting caught up with communication methodology caregivers must be emotionally prepared for their journeys to support the child's language and socio-emotional development. Getting support and feeling supported remain essential; some parents require more support and counsel, while others engage in supports naturally.

*Social*, *emotional*, and *informational* supports parents of children with hearing loss receive are therefore important, and they help parents feel connected, trust in relationships (and themselves), develop competencies, and become empowered. These supports move parents to the center of the constellation of support for their children. They help parents become primary influencers and leaders of their children's welfare.

***Social Supports:*** Social supports are relational and help maintain caregiver mental health. The connections parents have with others facing the same issues can reduce emotional stress and decrease feelings of loneliness and isolation. Positive relationships made with practitioners, other parents, persons with hearing loss, and people parents trust also help them cultivate perspective and nurture an ability to persevere.

***Emotional Supports:*** Parents build confidence when they believe themselves and feel capable of accomplishing a task and dealing with challenges. Being emotionally prepared to help their children can stem from positive social encounters. Practitioner empathy, parent groups, and family participation emotionally support parents in their journeys to parent and raise their children. Emotional support boosts parents' self-efficacy. (Refer to interventions in Part One.)

***Informational Supports:*** Parents who are informed have acquired knowledge that increases feelings of confidence and abilities to engage in their children's development. Information is empowering and guides parents to participate in productive ways that help their children. Informational supports include communication development and socio-emotional growth of children.

Finding social, emotional, and informational supports in low- and limited- resource environments is challenging. These supports address parent needs and the development of children's communication, learning, and potential. For this reason, practitioners are key influencers of caregivers' journeys and the educational and learning pathways of children. Though professionals acquire different knowledge and have specialized skills, they must help parents find essential supports that align with parent interests and needs. Practitioners can also explain and explore individualized services for their children.

All parent supports are important to the well-being of the family. Supports might be social connections parents have with others (**relational**). Supports help caregivers acknowledge their feelings (**emotional**) in response to hearing loss and stigma imposed by their environment. They help parents acquire knowledge (**informational**) that can be shared with relatives and neighbors. When parents are open to learning about hearing health and habilitation, more trusting in themselves, and engaged in meaningful relations, they become more empowered. Further, non-judgmental and compassionate supports help foster parent's willingness to trust in and feel good about available supports. Supports also help reduce negative perceptions and fears preventing caregivers from participating.

*Here are examples of social/relational supports:*

- Hearing health clinics/practitioners
- Schools for the deaf/teachers
- Churches
- Social Media (Facebook, WhatsApp)
- Social service centers
- Local and regional parent groups
- Parents and parent groups
- Family

*Here are examples of emotional supports:*

- Practitioners of Audiology
- Teachers of the Deaf
- Social workers
- Family members
- Friends and neighbors
- Parents of children with hearing loss
- Adults with hearing loss
- Children with hearing loss

*Here are examples of informational supports:*

- Websites: hearing aid, cochlear implant, hearing health organizations
- Parent Handbooks: how to guides, mainstream guides, etc.
- Parent workshops
- Webinars
- Educational materials: sign language, aural/oral, parenting, behavior management
- Social Media
- Books

Some of the examples above fall into multiple categories and support caregivers in one or more ways. For example, parent support groups are not only social and relational but also informational. Parents with internet access might tap into informational supports online that are also emotionally and socially supportive. Many parents use WhatsApp and other social media to gather information and feel connected. Some parents choose to travel or move to other cities for support; they sacrifice work and finances to obtain services for their children. They may rely on church donations or family supports to facilitate this option.

Informational, social, and relational supports are critical, yet they can be overwhelming. Parents need help filtering through information and supports that feel right. A solution for one child born to deaf parents may not apply to another child born to hearing parents. In low resource communities, peer contacts and meaningful relationships are vital to making sense of all the available supports. Most parents initially have no idea of available supports.

As practitioners explore essential ways to support caregivers, fostering their psychological well-being remains central. Positive psychology is no doubt helpful. Doing what works best for parents is crucial. Being optimistic about the future, feeling self-assured, and enjoying time with the child and family are positive aspects of parenting. The parents' psychological well-being becomes the foundation of their success. And caregivers who discover innate strengths and confidence help themselves grow in positive and healthy ways. As parents embody new knowledge, they become more determined to help their children succeed. Parents may cultivate their *best self* as they explore competencies and leadership skills.

Parents who are fully supported and informed can also emerge as change agents in their communities, even in small or indirect ways. They inform and educate people in their family, church, school, and workplace, which in turn can influence inclusion and understanding of children with hearing loss. Parents can also emerge as role models in their communities and families, providing social, informational, and relational supports to other parents and their families. They may also participate in or lead parent groups or become advocates for their children's rights. There is no telling what parents will do when they are fully informed and supported.

Needless to say, parent supports in low- and limited- resource communities are challenging but necessary. Progress for children occurs when positive supports help parents find ways to thrive in their journeys to raise their children. The quality of life for children with hearing loss often depends on their caregivers and their involvement. This is also influenced by how mentally and emotionally prepared caregivers are to care for the needs of their children.

> Although short term or intermittent, humanitarians on service missions also provide informational, relational, and social supports depending on the specific medical or educational objectives.
>
> Many families enlist in a hearing health mission each year to obtain new Hearing Assistive Technologies for their children. Families might receive brief lessons in how to use and care for the devices or ways to communicate with their children.
>
> Missions give families opportunities to mingle with other families. Every opportunity to bring parents together can be meaningful, especially if someone facilitates interaction and communication among the parents and children.

## Coaching and Empowering

"The greatest good you can do for another is not just to share your riches but to reveal to him his own." ~ Benjamin Disraeli

*Coaching* refers to ways of inspiring and elevating people to unlock personal potential. The process for practitioners involves asking parents questions at the right time, helping them reflect on their situations and guiding them to evaluate options that are supportive to the outcome they seek. Coaching focuses on personal development and informational support that encourages parents to visualize a clear path and the goals for their children. Rather than directing a parent to address a list of instructions, coaching fosters independent thinking and awareness of what needs to happen.

Coaching should help parents become introspective, which can play a pivotal role in self-actualizing competencies and leadership qualities. Parents foster their well-being when they take a healthy and positive approach to self-examine their actions and abilities. Coaching parents, therefore, requires practitioners to support parents' self-learning and increase positive experiences. At the same time, coaching helps parents to understand the quality care and services their children need and to acquire knowledge pertinent to the children's development. Good coaching leads parents to make informed decisions and be responsive to their children's learning. Good coaching builds parent capacity and leads parents to become empowered and active participants in their children's progress.

Key elements of coaching include empathetic listening, optimism, positive support, and questioning that explores clients and their family contexts. Developing a partnership with parents, listening intently to their personal scenarios, and informing parents at levels commensurate with their comprehension and abilities are important. Being compassionate, attentive, and truthful nurtures calm in parents who may feel overwhelmed and stressed.

*Empowerment* can be defined as the process that encourages people to take their own affairs in hand and to discover their own capabilities. At the same time, empowerment allows people to learn and appreciate the solutions that they have worked out for themselves (cf. Rappaport, 1987). Empowered parents of children with hearing loss need to feel confident in their position as caregivers. Parents want to help their children communicate and learn. They need informational, social, and emotional supports that are encouraging and build self-assurance. And when they receive guidance from experienced and knowledgeable practitioners, they walk on the path of self-discovery and self-determination.

## *Approaches to Coach and Empower Caregivers*

Serving caregivers of children with hearing loss is a practitioner's most important and primary role. The needs of every child are unique, and every parent is the inroad to a child's success. Parent support to understand childhood hearing loss, technology, and communication development are just as important as strategies for self-care, personal growth, and parenting skills. Coaching caregivers, therefore, requires planning and asks practitioners to consider the following:

- Identify parental attitudes and beliefs, and then expand parent perspective.

- Generate deep knowledge and learning about hearing loss and communication opportunities across the range of populations.

- Listen empathically and attune to caregiver emotions, desires, and needs.

- Lead conversations with the character strengths of caregivers.

- Explore ways parents can nurture their children's development in their homes.

- Nurture caregiver understanding of the challenges they face.

- Explain disability laws and the children's rights to inclusion and learning.

- Inform parents of their responsibilities in non-directive ways.

- Help parents seek out and identify all educational supports.

# Empathetic Listening

"The first stage of learning is silence; the second stage is listening." ~ Maori proverb

In the developing world, practitioners might have little time to sit and listen to lengthy stories. Long lines of people waiting for hearing tests and hearing aid repairs prevent prolonged conversations. Short therapy sessions for children and home visits may only allow for limited consultation and time with families. However, parents need support and want to be coached. They also want to be heard.

Allowing time for parents to express their thoughts and needs is important. This gives permission for parents to state their beliefs and opinions about their children, family situations, and hearing loss. They engage in the learning process as they sort through their thoughts, knowledge, and concerns. Giving parents time to talk and lead the conversation helps practitioners counsel with relevancy.

*ATTUNEMENT*... tuning in and attending fully to incoming streams of information without becoming carried away by preconceived ideas or perceptual biases (Daniel Siegal, 2010).

*RESONANCE*... joining together, coach being one with a coachee, a borrowing of energy, or level of presence with one another.

Practitioners can be a lifeline for parents, and the relationships that are built remain vital to parents' successes and children's development. Practitioners might be the only contact parents may have as they navigate their children's hearing loss. In many low- and limited- resource countries, teachers of the deaf or audio technicians, for example, might be the only professionals knowledgeable about children's hearing. When practitioners attune to parent attitudes, feelings, thoughts, and interpretations, their relationships with families are improved. A stronger alliance is formed when practitioners are empathetic listeners, attend to parent needs, and invite parents as partners of their children's development.

Being a good listener strengthens the relationship, builds trust, and further facilitates a practitioner's ability to address the priorities of parents and how they can help their children. When fully attuned to the energies of another, the intrapersonal relationship is culminated with reciprocal, mutual, and collaborative communication. Science continues to study the energy between people and brain communication; brains are designed to interact with other brains.[79] Any opportunity to fully listen and attune to parents becomes essential.

# ENGAGED LISTENING ASSESSMENT

Being fully engaged in communication involves listening to others' views, feelings, interpretations, and values concerning the content. It requires patience and focus. In engaged listening, both parties are given the opportunity to fully express themselves.

Below is a list of listening blocks, behaviors that prevent us from being fully engaged in the conversation. Read each statement and place a ✓ in the column that best describes your use of the listening block. Be honest with yourself!

| Listening Block | Yes | No | Sometimes |
| --- | --- | --- | --- |
| 1. I give others advice when they really just want to share information with me. | | | |
| 2. I pretend to listen to others while thinking of something else off-topic. | | | |
| 3. I dismiss what others say by minimizing what they believe to be true, i.e., "You're overreacting," "You'll be fine," "It's not a big deal," etc. | | | |
| 4. I use others' conversational information as an opportunity to share what has happened to me that might be similar. | | | |
| 5. While on the telephone, I find myself doing other things rather than fully paying attention. | | | |
| 6. When I am in a meeting and my phone rings, I answer it. | | | |
| 7. I interrupt or try to finish others' sentences. | | | |
| 8. I jump to conclusions and react when someone is talking. | | | |
| 9. I make up my mind before I have all the information. | | | |
| 10. I am a compulsive note taker, which prevents me from getting the full story. | | | |
| 11. I am impatient. | | | |
| 12. I lose my temper when hearing things with which I don't agree. | | | |
| 13. I try to change the subject to something that relates to my own experiences. | | | |
| 14. I think more about my reply while the other person is speaking than what he or she is saying. | | | |

Engaged Listening Assessment created for Partners for A Greater Voice by Virginia Maglio, M.S., Learning and Development Consultant, 2017.

## A Note to Practitioner:

Practitioners must open their hearts and minds and listen closely to the family members they support. Parent needs can change from day to day, and sometimes just being there to listen, console, or encourage is all that matters. Putting aside personal perspectives and professional agendas may also be needed. It is helpful when practitioners understand the various stages of family and child development as well as evolving levels of parental comprehension. Remaining empathic to parents is important and noticing their non-verbal and verbal cues can help.

Parents listen to the advice and counsel of practitioners, but there are times when they withdraw or seem frustrated. Parent body language can indicate when they have had enough information for one day, and if they feel overwhelmed. Practitioners can shift the conversation, reiterate what has already been discussed, or continue to educate parents during another meeting. There are some parents who are eager to learn and hear more, and these parents may be sitting on the edge of their seat and leaning into the conversation.

Practitioners should use a calming tone of voice, even when their personal agenda is demanding. Using positive, supportive language helps. There may be times when practitioners feel frustrated, which sometimes comes across as less available or interested in the parents. Trusting relationships are not built when practitioners are impatient or show frustration. If practitioners become aware of these behaviors, then they can reach out to colleagues to help them work through their feelings.

Parents know their children and want to learn how to help their children. They may not know what questions to ask or how to start a conversation around the needs of their children. For this reason, questioning parents is important. Their answers give clues to practitioners and help them to understand the parent experience and the family context. Parent comments help guide practitioners to offer relatable information. And when practitioners actively listen, parents learn that their opinion matters. Sometimes, a simple question can inspire parent ideas and their critical role in their children's learning and development. Questions can deepen the conversation with parents, and to encourage ways to empower parents.

Here are some questions practitioners might ask themselves:

> *How best does this family member learn? (aural/oral, visual, kinesthetic)*
>
> *What questions can I ask of parents that help me understand their personal story?*
>
> *What character strengths do I witness in the parents I work with?*
>
> *How can I encourage parents to be reflective, independent, and collaborative?*
>
> *What information can I offer that resonates with parents and supports their responsiveness to their children's communication and learning?*

Consider the Questions for Reflection below to deepen the conversation and to encourage ways to engage and empower parents.

> ### QUESTIONS FOR REFLECTION
>
> Questioning encourages critical thinking and accountability when practitioners pose questions that relate to the family context and children's needs. Questions help parents think about their children's welfare, especially when ideas and goals are generated from their responses. Some examples of questions that promote critical thinking and encourage caregiver feelings of empowerment include:
>
> *What is the vision you have for the future of your child?*
>
> *What do you want for your child socially and emotionally?*
>
> *What is a typical day-to-day routine for your child?*
>
> *What are some hobbies you do with your child?*
>
> *What do you most like about your typical day?*
>
> *How do you encourage your child's independence?*
>
> *What role does your child have in chores and day-to-day activities?*
>
> *How do you feel about that situation right now?*
>
> *What do you love about your child?*
>
> *Tell me more about the behavior of your child at home.*
>
> *How do you respond to your child when he is trying to communicate?*

# Relationships

"Let us be grateful to the people who make us happy; they are the charming gardeners who make our souls blossom." ~ Marcel Proust

Our lives are enriched by the connections we have with other human beings. We learn and grow from meeting and interacting with others. Positive and supportive relationships can help us to feel healthier, happier, and more satisfied with ourselves and our lives.

Parents are key influencers of a child's quality of life and development, and they need positive and supportive relationships that make them feel good about themselves and their journeys to care for their children. When parents feel connected to practitioners they trust and who give positive encouragement to learn, grow, and develop, parents engage in a healthy outlook. And when parents and practitioners join together in support of their children, it forms an alliance that can be very empowering. Practitioners inform parents about the hearing health and communication needs of their children, helping parents to build competences and enabling them to become responsive to the care their children need. Parents inform practitioners of the challenges they face at home or in the learning their children need as well. Practitioners value opportunities to support the parent and promote the child's welfare.

**Parent Survey:**

The Partners for A Greater Voice survey found that the majority of parents living in the United States feel comfortable talking about their needs (51%) and the needs of their children (over 73%) with audiologists and doctors. In the Dominican Republic, parents also feel most comfortable talking with audiologists and teachers about the needs of their children (over 80%).

Parents are blessed with support when they have opportunities to learn from and be coached by doctors, therapists, and teachers. Because there are few practitioners in low- and limited- resource communities whom parents can rely on for ongoing support, parents may need to consider all relationships that will support them. Quality time with others remain vital for parents. Parents should cultivate positive and supportive relationships with neighbors, friends, and family members.

Positive parent-to-parent relationships offer important social, emotional, and informational supports to parents. When parents interact with other parents who are knowledgeable and share the same values and aspirations, parents discover they are not alone in the nurturing care they must give to their children. Shared parenting experiences, and helpful narratives from others who cope with hearing loss, help parents to understand what is required. The emotional journey and the resilient path are often discovered among parent-to-parent relationships. Parents also gain perspective on what is possible and attainable. Their stories may reveal struggles, successes, and practical ways to help children at home. As a result, parents develop competence and assurance in the help they give to their children.

Socialization prevents parents from retreating into isolation and instead encourages meaningful encounters which support parental well-being. And supportive, informational relationships are needed to empower parents and engage them in their children's development. Parents learn from others who are experienced in hearing health and habilitation, and they transfer what they hear and see to parenting their own children with hearing loss. And when parents are embraced with encouragement and positivity, they are inspired and want to learn more strategies and develop skills that aptly help their children.

## A Note to Practitioner:

The quality of life for a parent might be contingent upon relationships with family, friends, neighbors, and practitioners. Though most parents are comfortable talking with practitioners, some may have limited access to practitioners and may not be able to solely rely on them for support. A network of like-minded parents may not exist, or they live far from professional services. Therefore, parents need to build and nurture positive, feel good relationships. Even when these may be inconsistent or imperfect, positive and supportive relationships are essential and can help parents thrive and feel good about themselves. Their journeys may be happier when people who love and care for them are in their lives.

Parents are more likely able to cope, make informed decisions, and find services that support their children's needs when their relationships inspire them to move forward. Discrimination, potential abuse, and slander can hinder their progress. Although it may be challenging for parents in low- and middle- resource communities to reach outside their family and current network of friends, it might be necessary for parents to seek out new relationships. A positive mindset becomes stronger when relationships are emotionally supportive.

Based on stigma and difficulties that families face in resource poor communities, practitioners can help parents to recall experiences and relationships that make them feel good and encourage them to be their best. Family, friends, and neighbors affect parents' well-being. They need experiences that induce positive self-perceptions and acknowledge their abilities. It becomes important for practitioners to apply strategies that unburden the hearts of parents and which enable parents to develop meaningful, positive relationships with not only their children but with themselves and others.

Practitioners can ask parents how they feel when interacting with their children and a family member. What everyday moments do parents appreciate? Encouraging moments of joy and positive relational experiences can help parents move forward in positive ways. Use the exercise on the next page to help parents cultivate and maintain positive, supportive, and joyful relationships.

# EXERCISE MOMENTS OF JOY

Discuss the times parents experience positive relationships and pleasure in their lives. Ask parents to think about some of the ways they *most enjoy* gathering with family and friends - the moments that make them feel good. Don't have parents ponder for too long; have them list instances that first come to mind.

Encourage parents to weave moments of joy into their lives as often as possible.

1.

2.

3.

4.

5.

6.

7.

8.

9.

10.

# ENCOURAGING PARENT/CHILD INTERACTION

According to Gerald Mahoney, a professor of Families and Communities at Case Western Reserve University, "parents and caregivers are the major influence on their children's development. The effectiveness of therapy interventions is highly associated to progress when parents are more responsive with their children and during a course of early intervention" (2009).[80] Early interventionists and child development specialists agree that parent and child interaction during real life activities and routines is key to promoting children's communication and socio-emotional growth. And when parents do this with a positive mindset, and with strengths and leadership skills in mind, the opportunities to help their children learn and progress are even greater.

Encouraging parent/child interactions involves helping parents approach their children in natural ways. This involves helping parents to develop skills that nurture their children's language, learning, and conduct. According to research, mothers are more likely to be highly engaged when interventions address child development and when practiced in a learning environment. Skill development has proven to be more successful than when parents are told what to do in a conversation.[81] Dathan Rush, CCC-SLP, a speech-language pathologist, summarizes the important steps that practitioners should consider in their coaching practice:

- *Observing* the parent and child engaged in the typical routine or activity and, if necessary, giving the parent an opportunity to learn from observing the practitioner model a new strategy with the child,

- Giving the parent opportunities to *practice* new strategies with the child,

- Prompting the parent's *reflection* on what is or isn't working (and why) and generating new ideas,

- Providing *feedback* by sharing ideas and information,

- *Joint planning* with the parent on their work between visits to foster child learning and prepare for the next visit. [82]

Across the field of speech, language, and child development, fostering parent-child interaction in their natural environment is often necessitated. Everyday routines at home are important opportunities for parents to engage with their children and nurture their learning and communication. The knowledge parents acquire may be more meaningful when it links it to their experiences at home. Because parents spend a lot of time attending to chores, work, and celebrations, they might respond favorably to advice with these things in mind. Practitioners often bridge daily routines with ways parents can nurture their children's language, socio-emotional growth, and inclusion. Activities at home are opportunities for parents to interact with their children and promote language-learning opportunities. Children are curious and want to learn. They need parents to play with them, nurture them, and lead them to discover the world in natural and fun ways. Whether washing dishes, doing laundry, or cooking a meal, parents should be encouraged to invite their children to help and to teach them everything they are doing.

## *Challenges in developing countries*

There are many situations in developing countries that affect parents' well-being and participation in their children's progress. Basic needs such as food, clothing, and shelter are often priorities for families living in low resource communities. Caring for many children under one roof, poor health, and limited finances are a few other obstacles parents face, economically and emotionally. These realities often prevent families from finding enough time to nurture their children and develop their children's communication and learning.

How to manage children's moods and behaviors is also challenging for parents and disconcerting. The abuse and neglect of children with hearing loss is a reality. Parents are often unaware of the consequences of the socio-emotional physical, psychological, cognitive, and behavioral development of children when they don't interact with their children or are abusive. Parenting skills are needed to nurture and care for children with hearing loss. Parenting education and training is essential. Workshops can help parents to know the importance of being gentle, kind, and loving with children who have hearing loss. Simply knowing this fact can help parents to think about ways they interact with their children and remain compassionate.

Further, there might be few practitioners to serve thousands of people seeking hearing health, and such support given to children and their parents is precious. The absence of enough technical expertise and educational services for children makes it especially difficult for practitioners who face a large population of families alone. This means that every meeting with a caregiver becomes an essential opportunity to discuss caregiver strengths and nurture them in distinct ways, and as early in the child's life as possible.

## *Comments on Critical Thinking:*

Clearly, practitioners want to share ideas and advise; they know the value of informing caregivers. They want to support parent journeys and help them be attentive to their children's hearing, language, and development. Coaching caregivers is complex, and counsel must attune to the family context. It is a process and evolves over time. Importantly, parents need to be ready to hear and put into practice what they learn. Often, the application of knowledge, skills, and determination is best fostered when parents learn to think for themselves.

"Critical thinking is self-directed, self-disciplined, self-monitored, and self-corrective thinking. It entails effective communication and problem-solving abilities. (wikipedia)" One way to foster critical thinking skills is to help parents think of situations that require them to examine possible outcomes. Consider the exercise below.

# "IF THEN?" EXERCISE

The IF THEN? exercise involves every day scenarios that parents easily relate to and can be a springboard for reasoning, conversation, and decision-making. Facilitators of this exercise can identify problems that parents are currently facing and develop "IF THEN" scenarios to help them think about and evaluate the outcomes.

Here are some examples:

> "IF you teach your child a routine or provide structure at home, THEN what do you expect will happen with your child's behavior?"

> "IF your child does not wear the hearing aids consistently, THEN what will happen to her ability to learn to listen and understand spoken language?"

> "IF you routinely involve your child and explain everything you are doing, THEN how will your child feel?"

The IF THEN? exercise is practical and relatable. Scenarios help parents to think about their own environment, their actions, and how it affects their children's learning and development. It is easy to administer to individual parents or to groups of parents. When "IF THEN" examples are shared in a group setting, parents listen to real life commentary. Parents might learn about the benefits of establishing routines, interacting with their children, supporting socio-emotional growth, and encouraging hearing aid use. Parents might also evaluate and explore how they interact with their children and discover how their children learn from watching and modeling them.

## A Note to Practitioner:

Parents learn differently and move at different paces. Empowering caregivers is a process, and practitioners must be patient, open-hearted, and mindful of the parents' learning journeys. Conversations about hearing health care and the importance of children's learning and communication must inevitably remain positive. Whenever possible, informing parents must extend beyond hearing health care instructions and guide parents to realize their parenting capacity, innate character strengths, and intuition. The support parents are given should always encourage ways parents feel good about themselves and their decisions. And when parents' psychological well-being is nurtured, parents may engage more intentionally and happily in their journeys to parent their children.

When parents are encouraged to explore their innate potential and are given strategies that align with their abilities to help their children, it leads to parent feelings of self-confidence and competence. Their behavior is fundamentally rooted in feelings of worth, self-awareness, and human potential.[83] With character strengths of love, hope, perspective, and curiosity, parents might include their children in daily chores, social experiences, and community activities. A strength of bravery gives parents courage to bring their children to church and other events in their town. A strength of humor invites children to laugh and have fun learning to cook, getting dressed, playing, and doing other tasks at hand. Most often, parents need positive, nurturing experiences with their children before discovering how their rapport greatly influences their children's development.

### *Communication Tips:*

How does effective communication with parents influence the way parents feel about themselves, approach their children's development, and actively engage in services and supports? The list of all the things a practitioner must explain to parents can be lengthy. What comes first, second, and third? Parents may forget or become easily confused by large amounts of information on hearing aids, language development, and ear care. How practitioners approach and communicate with caregivers is very important. Here are some communication tips for practitioners:

- use uplifting language
- keep your voice calm
- acknowledge parent difficulties
- use open-ended questions
- acknowledge what parents say
- make time for silence so parents can think for themselves
- ask parents to reiterate what you say

# Coaching Parents on Communication Opportunities

Communication opportunities are the avenues for children with hearing loss to learn language, socialization, basic word knowledge, and vocabulary. The modality, whether visual or spoken, becomes the vehicle for literacy and communication. Parents have a right to choose a mode of communication, and parent involvement is essential. They need to understand communication opportunities and the importance of immersing their children in the language of choice.

Supporting parents' decision is imperative. Practitioners should employ best practices and educate parents on all the ways children with hearing loss can learn and communicate. Best practices are professional procedures, guidelines, and principles that provide the best possible care for patients.[84] Whether or not a country or a school mandates a particular communication opportunity, options do exist. These are the three primary communication opportunities that parents need to understand:

- Signed Language (visual / manual language)

- Aural/Oral Communication (auditory-verbal / listening and spoken language)

- Bi-lingual Communication / Signed Supported Spoken Language (both sign and spoken language are combined)

Sign, aural/oral, and signed supported communication opportunities have extensive history. Most people are biased toward a communication opportunity, and their training or exposure to one method over another may influence why one approach may be recommended to children. Rather than impose a communication method, practitioners are encouraged to explain all communication opportunities to parents as soon as their children's hearing levels are identified. They should share what they know with parents, limiting the bias they show toward one specific method. Even when communication opportunities do not appear to be available in the community, it is important to explain that options exist.

Parents have the right to decide on a communication approach that aligns with their beliefs and lifestyle, yet PGV has found most parents in low resource communities do not fully comprehend communication opportunities and what is required of them. Practitioners might tell parents communication opportunities exist, but they may not fully understand the intricacies of each methodology. Specialists and therapists knowledgeable or trained in an approach can help practitioners become more versed. They can in turn inform parents more adeptly on all ways children with hearing loss can communicate and learn language. The discussion should include expectations for children's development and learning needs, as well as details about the communication method.

In many low- and limited- resource communities, children with hearing loss face many challenges in their ability to learn and communicate freely and easily. Many of these children are unable to communicate at levels comparable to hearing peers and experience significant delays in language, speech, and socio-emotional growth. Children need access to information and a considerable amount of experience in developing their full potential. Communication development is especially important and necessary for children with hearing loss. Communicating helps people to express their ideas and feelings. It helps people to understand emotions and thoughts of others. Communication plays a vital role in life, and for children with hearing loss it demands parent and family involvement.

> Best practices are professional procedures, guidelines, and principals that provide the best possible care for patients and are accepted as being most effective for diagnosis and treatment (*Best Practices in Patient-Centered Care*, Conference Proceedings; Johns Hopkins University, 2013).

**Sign language** is a visual-manual modality of communication that involves hands and other body movements, including facial expressions and postures of the body, to convey meaning. Visual-manual communication develops naturally in low resource communities when parents use gestures and "home" signs. Visual-manual forms of communication are different across the world, and there is no universal sign language. While the number is not known exactly, over 300 kinds of sign languages may exist. Language fluency in visual-manual communication is more successful when taught by people who are skilled in the sign language of the region. Many Schools for the Deaf offer sign language classes and supports to families. Parents who enroll in sign language classes and get professional support to learn their local sign language can successfully communicate visually with their children. Parents and their children, in essence, learn visual-manual communication together.

**Aural/oral communication** is an approach that is used to describe listening and spoken language. Aural means hearing, and oral means spoken language. An aural/oral approach might infuse lipreading and gestures to facilitate spoken language. The method encompasses access to Hearing Assistive Technologies (HAT) and auditory based language-learning. Success in a mostly or fully auditory approach maximizes use of hearing to develop speech. This is most successful when children are diagnosed at a young age, appropriate supports are available to parents, and services maximize auditory skill development. Children learn to speak when they practice learning to listen and wearing their HAT consistently. Their success may be based on how often parents speak naturally and model language, as well as enrollment in auditory-based language services. Individual auditory-verbal therapy supports the needs of children and engages parents in their children's development. Parents learn about aural/oral communication and language development in therapy sessions and can apply strategies at home. Refer to the Supplement on PGV's comments on aural/oral communication for further information.

**Bi-lingual communication**, more recently termed *signed supported spoken language*, combines both aural/oral and manual communication approaches. In many low- and limited- resource countries, bi-lingual communication is a recommended form of communication for children with any degree of hearing loss. For children developing language, exposure to bi-lingual communication can be confusing when neither access to signs or spoken language are consistent. Bi-lingual communication requires intensive work using an aural/oral approach supported with visual signs and gestures. Children can fully develop a complete language with consistent exposure. Parents must understand that a manual form of communication supports spoken language outcomes and requires good auditory access with HAT.

There is a learning curve with every methodology, and parents need access to information about each one. Good coaching and instruction on any chosen method must ensure parents have the necessary skills to help their children communicate and develop language. The methodology of choice should be a good fit for their children and their families. Some parents choose one method at first and then shift to another. The important message to instill in the minds and hearts of parents is immersion in an accessible language. Preferably in the very early years of a child's life, parents need to develop skills in the method of choice in order to successfully help their children.

Practitioners must respect and support the parent choice. The decisions parents make go hand in hand with their beliefs, culture, and the vision they have for their children. Hearing parents often choose aural/oral communication because it is the method most natural to their hearing environment, but this should not prohibit parents from choosing other options. Ultimately parents must act on behalf of their children until they can make their own decisions, even when the communication method may not come naturally or easily. Even when communication opportunities do not appear to be available in the community, practitioners must find ways to support and inform parents about all options.

Parents need time to process new information in hearing health and how they can support their children's communication and learning, especially when their children are first diagnosed with hearing loss. The unfamiliar path can be frightening and potentially threatening to their social environment and **locus of control**.[85] Information given to parents may be overwhelming at first, and that knowledge takes time for them to absorb and comprehend. Parents need to feel capable and confident in their communication choice as well as ability to engage in their children's communication development. Spoken or signed language often entails spending more time with their children than with other children in the family. It may necessitate practitioner meetings and workshops where parents can explore communication opportunities, decide which method works best for their children, and develop related skills.

Once parents are informed about communication opportunities, they can explore all available resources and supports. Children's communication and learning should not be delayed, and when parents discover resources and available supports, they eagerly engage in helping their children. Personal resources and character strengths are helpful. For example, when parents are aware of their psychological capital and use their innate strengths, they may interact with their children and others more intentionally and energetically. A strength of perseverance or love can motivate parents to help their children learn and grow. With a strength of curiosity, parents may research and explore education and language development. Parents need to feel confidence in the communication approach and believe in their abilities and skills. Their success is contingent upon supports that foster their capacity to parent and which can guide them further.

> **Locus of Control** is "the degree to which people believe that they have control over the outcome of events in their lives, as opposed to external forces beyond their control" (wikipedia). The concept first described by Julian B. Rotter in 1954 suggests, "People with a high internal locus of control believe in their own ability to control themselves and influence the world around them." People may see their future as being in their own hands and that their own choices can lead to success or failure.

Ultimately, coaching parents should broaden parent knowledge and expand perspective. The application of information must align with parents' expectations and unlimiting beliefs. At the same time, coaching must raise the bar for children's potential while influencing parent accountability.

## A Note to Practitioner:

Informing parents about communication opportunities is essential and requires practitioners to become knowledgeable and accepting of all methodologies. Too often, practitioners assume parent choice or that the cultural environment or past support given to other children in the community is what is called for. Practitioners should limit bias and embrace the parent interest. Practitioner coaching should align with parents' beliefs and vision they have for their children. The conversation between practitioner and parent must address caregiver perceptions and expectations while supporting the child's learning and communication.

Practitioners can use their most dominant character strengths to communicate with parents and help them find supports they need to make decisions. For example, practitioners can apply a strength of honesty or zest to express what they know about a methodology and offer as many suggestions as possible. Strengths of love of learning (gather knowledge about a method), self-regulation (remain emotionally neutral and objective), judgement (being open-minded about choices), and other strengths can be useful to apply here.

There may be occasions practitioners need to refer parents to others who have more experience in speech and language or expertise in the local sign language. And whenever possible, practitioners should encourage parents to meet other parents in their community who have experience or knowledge in sign language, aural/oral, and bi-lingual communication. Meeting others is informative and can be motivating for parents. They often engage in a communication opportunity when they gain knowledge about it and see how other children with hearing loss learn language and make progress.

Parent groups, books, videos, and classes on communication opportunities can also be helpful. Many online resources, pamphlets, and parent guides can further support the parent choice. Several manufactures of Hearing Assistive Technologies (HAT) and global health organizations offer free information and brochures on communication opportunities that can be downloaded and printed. These resources can be explained or given to parents. Culturally relevant flyers can also be developed should practitioners choose to create them.

# What Do Parents Want?

In over 35 international missions and 1000 encounters with parents, Partners for A Greater Voice (PGV) has witnessed the parent heart and mind. Results from a parent education survey conducted in 2015 specify parent desires and interests.

Parents want to believe that their children can succeed. They want their children to be independent, happy, and included in their communities and schools. In many low resource communities, parents often say they want their children to marry and to get a job. Though parents often question the cause of hearing loss, they seek support to know how to best care for their children's hearing and ability to talk and communicate. They want to know that they have the skills to help their children succeed in their communities.

Parents often lean into the experience of others. They often feel they are alone in their journeys and look to practitioners for guidance. Practitioners are resourceful and skilled, and parents often trust and rely on their expertise. They often want someone else to help them solve a problem or challenge they face. Parent behavior might include "handing the problem off to someone else." Culture, class, family pressures, or grief may trigger this behavior. Parents often want practitioners to simply tell them what to do.

Results from the 2015 survey indicate the majority of parents in the Dominican Republic want to be trained and learn how best to care for their children. More than 85% of these parents say they desire more formal training and education, with the overwhelming majority of them willing to attend workshops when offered in their community. More than 170 responses indicated interest in the following topics:

- appropriate hearing technologies
- listening and spoken language
- mainstream education
- behavior management
- ways I can teach my child
- activities at home to help my child
- how to interact with family members
- how to advocate for my child
- how to support socio-emotional development of my child

Parents say they mostly receive information on causes of hearing loss, degrees of hearing loss, Hearing Assistive Technologies (HAT), and activities at home to help their children. Parents want more information on cochlear implants, teaching children to listen and talk, anatomy of the ear, and sign language. They are also interested in disability laws, mainstreaming children in society and schools, and how to defend and advocate for their children. *Subject matters parents primarily want more of include developing resilience, learning about their emotions, caring for their children's social and emotional growth, managing children's behavior, and starting parent groups.*

Based on this PGV survey, it seems clear that parents are interested in a broad range of topics. It becomes the job of the practitioner to source what matters most to parents and to address their curiosities. Creating an informal survey, developing a check list of topics, or asking parents what they want to learn more about are approaches to exploring parent interests and desires. Informational and relationship supports therefore must relate to parents' unique situations and offer practical advice that targets parents' interest. Empowering parents ultimately facilitates ways parents embrace their responsibilities to care for, nurture, and make decisions for their children.

Surprisingly, only 6% of parents say they learn about hearing loss from parents, even though over 55% *believe* they can learn the most from other parents (phone, face-to-face, parent consultants). When parents are asked to rank what would best support their social and emotional needs, they say parent education, workshops, blogs, and websites ranked *lower* than regularly attended parent groups, informal conversations with other parents, support from doctors and teachers. Knowing that parents want to talk about their needs is encouraging. The interpersonal relationships they seek, therefore, need more attention.

## A Note to Practitioner:

Practitioners know how intensive and important parent education and supports are. When mentored and coached, parents become primary partners who learn and grow as competent caregivers of children with hearing loss. Parents must feel they are important team members and important influencers of their children's development. Teamwork among practitioners and parents become invaluable. Their collaboration provides both parent and practitioner with opportunities to learn about the family context, make decisions relevant to the children's social, emotional, and cognitive needs, and develop a plan of action. When collaboration becomes close and trustworthy, parents are more open to share their narratives, embrace a practitioner's suggestions, and assume their role in raising their children.

The practitioner's goal is to create partnerships with the caregivers. These relationships become essential in addressing the critical needs of children. Practitioners must envision parents as primary partners in the child's development and remain supportive to the parent learning journey. Practitioners must walk alongside the parents to guide and coach them. A reputable coaching approach is not authoritative and never dictates. The process involves compassionate rapport that essentially passes on information and ideas in timely and supportive ways.

# **Parent Support Groups**

Parent support groups are safe environments for learning. They are often described as the most valued experience among caregivers challenged with their journey to help children learn and communicate. Parent group meetings inform parents and can help them face stigma and reality. When parents attend a support group, they make meaningful connections with others who share similar experiences. The relationships parents develop are vital to parent learning and the discovery of pragmatic ways to support their children's communication and learning. These groups help parents feel connected in ways that help them persevere and cope. Feelings of isolation may decrease as a result. Whether there are five or fifty parents in a room, peer support groups engage parents and provide dynamic social, informational, and emotional supports.

One of the wonderful benefits of peer-to-peer interactions is the opportunity to hear parent stories and to learn practical ways to help children with hearing loss. Parents want their children to thrive and be included in all aspects of life, and the narratives parents share with each other provide insight and tangible, realistic strategies to take home. Parents like to tell their personal experiences and will do so when they trust the social environment. Seeing and hearing from other families gives parents something to reflect on and believe in.

The experiences parents share in conversation are invaluable and can help parents plan, make decisions, and solve challenges they may face at home. Educational placement, language development, behavior management, and hearing technologies are often subjects of interest that arise during parent support meetings, and through these discussions parents learn about the failures and achievements of other families and their children. These realities parents express in their stories are precious lessons. Peer-to-peer interactions allow parents to witness the common emotions of families, to understand children's rights for inclusion and education, and to learn ways to troubleshoot technology. As parents absorb all they hear and see, they develop a sense of security and connectedness. They learn to apply what they learn. They make decisions that are appropriate for their children and families as a result.

Science tell us interpersonal connections are vital to happiness (Diener & Biswas-Diener, 2008).[86] Parent group support can alleviate some of the emotional baggage that prevent parent engagement. Key skills parents learn in parent relationships include adapting new routines that support the child, expanding perspectives of a child's potential, and learning how to make decisions. Further, being absolved from the cause of hearing loss may be discovered. Empathy, trust, and vital feelings of connectedness emerge among parents when they come together. Parents learn how their emotion affect them, resulting in becoming more emotionally flexible.

In addition to this, parent groups can be powerful instruments of change. When parents bond, they learn they are more likely able to accomplish more together than alone. Parents advocate for their children's school accommodations and social inclusion. When they come together as a group, they may initiate or promote early childhood policy, early identification, mainstream education, and disability rights. Many parents become involved in hearing health and habilitation based on their interests; some train and study to be advocates, audiology technicians, teachers, or social workers. Their collective force is immeasurable.

The industry is often driven by parents when parents become partners in hearing health and habilitation. In Uganda, a father of a child with a cochlear implant is a driving force for fundraising and strategy to initiate a school for aural/oral education. In India, two parents collaborate to establish a parent network that reaches over 500 families. Even when parents do not become professionals in the industry, they can impact their communities in positive ways. A group of parents in the Dominican Republic bond to sell baked goods and products at the public beach to raise money for their children's school. Further, two mothers who are informed and trained in their children's hearing health provide outreach and support to other parents in their community, encouraging hearing aid use, school attendance, and their participation at parent group meetings. Parents can positively influence change.

### Parent Group Perspectives

Parenting children with hearing loss is a journey accompanied by a collection of beliefs, emotions, communication methodologies, and hearing heath practices. Parents fuel each other's learning, motivation, and exploration of solutions that help their children. Here are some benefits:

"Parent support meetings help me understand that my child's hearing loss does not define his character."

"Parent conversation makes me realize that I am not alone."

"Parents teach me ways to communicate with my child."

"I learn about mainstream education supports for my child at meetings."

"Not only do I feel supported, I gain a certain confidence that I need to parent my child the best way I know how."

"Groups of parents are my classroom."

"Narratives and shared experiences, good and bad, help me see the bigger picture."

"The more I meet with parents, the more insight and knowledge I acquire."

*Parent Group Challenges in the Developing World*

The absence of parent groups in many communities begs practitioners to find ways parents can come together. In low resources communities, regularly scheduled parent groups and attendance at parent meetings are challenging even when the meetings are free. It seems easy enough to invite and gather parents together since parent groups provide meaningful support on many levels (emotional, informational, relational), so why wouldn't they want to attend? In the developing world, many parents face sincere and difficult challenges that prevent them from participating. Depending on the culture and environment, practitioners may run up against multiple barriers that inhibit parent responsiveness to parent group participation.

Distance from home or work, traffic, and cost of transportation may hinder parents' ability to attend. Parents might stay home because of heavy rains or a child's illness. Family and work obligations also excuse parents from participating. Social stigma and poor perception of hearing loss could prevent parents from engaging with others outside the comfort of the family and community. Parents might hide their child in the home or feel too ashamed to associate with a disability group. Emotions and grief can block caregiver's good intentions to meet other parents. There are a dozen reasons why parents may not be willing to participate, yet there are far more advantages for parents to attend meetings and come together with others who share similar circumstances.

*Here are some benefits of parent groups:*

- fosters peer connectedness
- breaks down stigma
- stimulates learning
- embraces role models
- supports emotional journeys
- initiates advocacy projects
- empowers parents
- reveals personal resources
- fosters parent skills and competence
- supports self-development
- invites family members

In many countries, school policies demand parent attendance in parent group workshops and informational sessions. This authoritative approach may work, yet most parents need to feel they have a choice to participate. It takes perseverance and creative incentives to engage families in meaningful peer-to-peer relations, but once parents experience the benefits of getting together, they are more likely to stay involved. Here are some initial ideas to encourage and motivate parents:

- Focus conversations on the benefits of parent support groups.

- Solicit input from parents and choose topics they want to learn about.

- Encourage active and interested parents to help with planning or coordination of events.

- Ask parents to be a voice that encourages other parents to attend and be involved.

- Explore parent perceptions of parent group support in your community, and then reiterate the most important benefits. (Expand the above list of benefits).

- Establish a day, time, and location for parents to gather; consistently offer meetings regardless of whether two or 50 parents turn up (monthly, bi-monthly, seasonally).

- Post a simple, one-page flyer in your clinic or establishment and distribute it throughout your community: churches, hospitals, schools, social service organizations.

- Use incentives to draw parents to the event, such as free food, dance, music, a guest speaker, free hearing screenings, parenting materials, and free hearing health pamphlets.

- Find parents to facilitate an event or parts of an event. At every meeting, ask a parent to help; give them one or two tasks at first. There are plenty of things parents can manage, so find what they are comfortable doing.

Words of advice:

Discussion groups are not personal counseling sessions. Find a qualified counselor or psychologist who can help parents in private.

Stick to your agenda; don't allow the conversation to move away from the topic you planned and are focused on. Say, "That's a great topic. Would everyone like to discuss this at the next meeting?"

Every audiology clinic, hospital, and school setting is a seed from which parent groups can emerge. Parent support groups are learning opportunities for both practitioner and parents. *A detailed approach to starting parent groups can be found in the Supplement in Part Four. For more help starting or fostering parent groups contact Partners for A Greater Voice.*

**A Note to Practitioner:**

Practitioners are challenged with job responsibilities, tasks, and busy schedules that may not permit ample time to properly plan parent support meetings. Job responsibilities often take priority over coordinating and attending a parent meeting. However, the benefits can be enormous for both practitioner and parent. The success of parent groups is often contingent upon the involvement of a nucleus of engaged people, and this can begin with the initial aid and facilitation of a practitioner.

Planning and coordinating parent events requires commitment and determination. Initially, practitioners need to be ambitious in their efforts to bring parents together and empower them to spearhead future parent focused events. Offering group meetings on a consistent basis is important for long term impact on parent engagement and empowerment. As with any program implementation, the first few parent meetings can be intense. However, hard work to coordinate these meetings generally pays off. Once a process is established it becomes less time consuming. Parents will form an allegiance when encouraged and invited to do so, and there are often parents who are willing to assume a leadership role of a parent event or the parent group. It is essential that practitioners involve those parents in the planning and coordination of events and meetings as soon as possible.

Recruiting parents who are willing to take charge and spearhead support group meetings may require a bit of searching, and this might not happen until parent meetings are well established. In any parent group initiative, it is important to find motivated parents who have the aptitude and interest to be involved. Parents do not have to be literate or well educated; they just need the drive and ambition. Parents who are social in nature are potential leaders and facilitators, as are parents who value and appreciate parent connections. Those who possess character strengths of perseverance, leadership, teamwork, fairness, and zest for life may also be good leaders and coordinators of parent support groups.

Before starting a parent group, sit with others who share your interest and brain storm ideas for starting parent groups and motivating parents to attend. Find a dedicated practitioner or service provider to initially manage the project. There may be parents who want to help. Brain storming ideas with a small group of people at work and with a few parents can determine culturally relevant ways to establish a group, encourage parent attendance, and people's willingness to participate. Working with a core group of people is an enormous asset to jump-start a parent group; working as a team, even if only two or three people, can result in greater success. The burden does not have to fall solely on one person.

Because environments and culture are different, it is prudent to explore parent support group strategies with other practitioners and parents in your community. Working together is important because starting a parent group takes perseverance and patience. It takes people willing to invest time in the coordination and planning of informational and social gatherings. Collaboration and consistency are the primary goals to keep in mind.

Parent groups can and should involve multiple practitioners from different disciplines, including people from disability organizations, churches, and government institutions. Whether the cause is focused on child rights, inclusion, early intervention, health, early childhood education, access, or government policy, the contributions made collectively promote and advance society's response to social problems and the inclusion of children and their parents. Though developing countries are challenged with expertise across the field of disability, the creation of parent groups and collaboration among available practitioners can contribute in distinct and positive ways. Every collaboration has the propensity to expand services and parent support, including ways to support children and their unique learning needs.

Strong family engagement in parent groups, consequently, is a driving force for reducing stigma, fostering awareness of hearing loss, promoting inclusion and disability rights, and improving the healthy development of children. Establishing a parent group in your community brings families together, and parents learn that an organized unit of families is stronger together than alone. Their collective strengths also give rise to their success. As parents become knowledgeable and involved in a parent group, they may choose to support other parents and the on-going efforts of parent-to-parent activities. Hence, parents can be both a supportive parent to others and a parent who continues to learn.[87] The benefits of parent groups are enormous.

## PARENT SUPPORT GROUP EXAMPLE: V-CONNECT FOUNDATION

VConnect Foundation is a parent support group based in India for parents of children who have a hearing loss and whose interest is to mainstream children in a hearing society. The organization informs and engages families in supports to help children learn to listen and speak with the use of hearing assistive technologies (HAT) and auditory verbal interventions. As a not-for-profit organization, VConnect offers support and guidance to a cross section of families from varied backgrounds and income levels.

The purpose of VConnect Foundation is to empower, support, and guide parents in their journeys to mainstream their children as successful participants and contributing members of society. In the creation of platforms and parent networks, both real and virtual, the organization helps connect parents with experts, device companies, agencies, centers, clinics, hospitals, and educational institutions. They also provide forums for parents and children to interact with and draw support from each other. They have three areas of focus:

1. Connect parents with the entire eco-system that is involved in their children's progress and development.

2. Influence mainstream schools and organizations to create education and employment opportunities for children.

3. Conduct a series of activities and events for social interaction and holistic development of children which are conducted in an inclusive, non-judgmental environment, and which help children gain confidence and self-esteem to face the world.

The idea to start VConnect Foundation first came to mind during a visit to the Alexander Graham Bell Convention in the United States in 2004, where Vahishtai Daboo, an auditory therapist and parent of a child with profound hearing loss, met with Joanne Travers, Executive Director of Partners for A Greater Voice and parent of two children born with hearing loss. Joanne's first visit to Mumbai, India in 2007 supported Vahishtai and her interest to start a parent group. Fatema Jagmag, also parent of a child with profound hearing loss and a trained audiologist, teamed up with Vahishtai to establish VConnect officially. Both women became deeply involved in the hearing health field as practicing professionals. Starting VConnect was necessary to advance supports to families who did not have the resources or supports to help their children. Joanne consulted Vahishtai, and PGV's Essential Programs to Coach and Empower was offered at an international VConnect conference in 2017 to support their parent empowerment initiatives.

The success of VConnect leaders to empower other parents has grown over the last decade to serve more than 1000 families in 10 parent groups located throughout Maharashtra, as well as parts of India and Kenya. Seven people serve on the advisory board, and parent coordinators run local parent group meetings. Advisors may travel to these meetings to support an initiative. Each year, parents from all over the region come together as a larger support group. The organization and parents predominantly communicate via WhatsApp and Facebook.

# Reducing Barriers to Stigma of Hearing Loss

Harsh stigma and discrimination associated with hearing loss exists around the globe, even in advanced societies where hearing health services and educational resources are prevalent. The shame and grief parents face are real. Reducing barriers of shame and discrimination must also promote ways children with hearing loss can thrive and participate in their communities and schools. People's beliefs about children with hearing loss are influenced when they understand *hearing* and the difficulties that can arise in language development when hearing is compromised. Practitioners, parents, children, or any persons with disabilities can dismantle misperceptions of children with hearing loss by explaining communication opportunities and ways children with hearing loss learn and thrive. When people are outspoken in their communities and explain what is possible for these children, they affect people's perceptions.

Hearing health care and habilitation are multifaceted and beg practitioners, parents, and their children to become educators in their communities. Studies have shown how outreach and education in the community may increase coping and resilience in some families.[88] This involves awareness of children with hearing loss as able-bodied. Rather than focus on the barriers to their learning and communication, positive aspects of children's abilities and inclusion in society should be emphasized. The visibility of children who face physical, cognitive and other challenges is needed. Their participation in all aspects of life and their community becomes important. Society then learns what children with hearing loss are capable of. Their success in school, employment, and friendship helps people see the possibilities. Insight to children's potential, regardless of age or ability, begins with understanding that every child, regardless of hearing loss, can thrive.

Parent interventions, therefore, must empower caregivers and engage them in a process to become involved and be active leaders of their children's inclusion and development. Parents are the life line for their children, especially in places where there is inadequate access to early identification, audiological services, and education programs for the deaf and hard of hearing. When parents engage in their children's lives, include them in community events, and talk with schools and community members about their children's potential, greater acceptance and understanding may emerge.

Not all caregivers feel comfortable talking about hearing loss or advocating for their children, but many will immerse themselves in the needs of their children because they want them to learn and be included in society. They may also want others to understand their predicament. Depending on parent strengths and personality, parents can be positive forces in the advancement of hearing loss acceptance and children's healthy development. When parents are informed and feel confident, they can explain the facts on hearing loss and ways their children learn and communicate. And when parents apply their character strengths, they become an influential voice.

The accountability for breaking down barriers of shame and judgement does not solely rest on the shoulders of caregivers. Schools, churches, hospitals, and community members also have an obligation to become involved and embrace the needs of children with unique needs. Creating opportunities to educate the greater community about children's hearing loss is important. Yet, to improve the inclusion of children with hearing loss in the community, people outside the caregiver's circle must understand that all children have social, emotional, and cognitive needs.

Clearly there is value and importance to create programs or campaigns that educate and inform citizens about hearing loss. Initiatives should build an understanding of differences while fostering inclusion of all children in education and learning. There may be opportunities for practitioners to intentionally coach and guide parents, even in small ways, to help increase community awareness of the individual needs of their children.

## A Note to Practitioner:

Here are some disability awareness tips to help reduce stigma:

- Recognize unique abilities children have; change your mindset and then raise the bar higher for their achievement.

- Recognize the knowledge parents have and their desires; be supportive of their unique journeys and never stop teaching them.

- Focus on a process to educate the public on disability and hearing loss; involve as many parents and people in your community as possible.

- Go beyond the facts of hearing loss and build awareness about people with hearing loss working and participating in society; provide information that encourages positive perceptions.

- Involve persons with hearing loss in awareness projects and community events to strengthen positive perceptions and their abilities.

- Reach out to organizations and professionals who can support awareness in any sector of health, socio/emotional growth of children, and well-being.

- Acknowledge disability policy on inclusion and education for children; share this knowledge with parents.

- Talk about the Convention for Rights of Persons with Disabilities (CRPD); consider hosting a parent meeting to discuss your country's policy and movement on disability rights (refer to Supplement I).

- Consider how stigma, limited beliefs, and discrimination can affect people's attitudes; engage in conversations about this to influence positive change.

# Fostering Hearing Loss Awareness in Schools

There is a great need in nearly all communities to promote an understanding of hearing health, hearing assistive technologies, and the inclusion of children with hearing loss in society. Audiology clinics, medical institutions, disability service organizations, parent groups, and parents contribute greatly to informing the general public. Noise pollution, aging populations affected by hearing loss, and disease that can manifest into hearing loss are all relevant subjects that apply to all people. These are important to any campaign for awareness.

Grass roots movements in schools can be an important means to promote an understanding of hearing loss among children. Targeting this population influences their perceptions and future sensitivities. Hearing peers can be accepting; their empathy can be developed at very young ages. They love learning about hearing loss prevention, hearing assistive technologies, communication opportunities, and positive ways children with hearing loss can participate in all aspects of life at school. Targeting the younger population makes sense, since children with hearing loss will grow up with them in their communities. Awareness programs implemented in schools often help children feel more connected.

Respect and compassion for children with hearing loss originates from a core understanding of possibility and ability, and a good place to get started is in schools and with school children who have typical hearing. When these children learn about hearing loss prevention, assistive technologies, language development, and ways people with hearing loss communicate, they come to a greater understanding of hearing loss. Children learn to appreciate ways people with hearing loss can communicate and succeed. Hearing loss may be understood as a difference rather than the identity of the person.

Awareness programs implemented in schools typically involve people knowledgeable about hearing loss, communication development, and hearing assistive technologies. This can include adults with hearing loss. All available stakeholders must be willing to visit schools and meet with school children. They should be non-biased in communication approaches and motivated to influence a positive environment for children with hearing loss. Such awareness involves mini educational sessions to inform school children and reduce barriers to their inclusion in society. These educational programs are particularly helpful in communities where there is a prevalence of people with hearing loss.

Practitioners and parents need to find time and be willing to step outside their comfort zone to foster an awareness and understanding of hearing loss in schools. Small projects or campaigns on hearing loss facts, hearing assistive technologies, or successful experiences of people living with hearing loss will broaden children's and teacher's understanding and acceptance. Further, school children often express what they learn at school to their family and neighborhood friends. An informed community realizes children with hearing loss are children first and have every right to be included in education, employment, and society.

Understanding the communication needs of children with hearing loss, their hearing assistive technologies, and their access to an education ideally involves professional training given to teachers and education specialists by practitioners in hearing health and habilitation. Referred to as In-Service, this professional development is especially important to support mainstreamed children with hearing loss enrolled in public or private schools. Most teachers lack specialized training and skills to serve diverse populations. It is a blessing if resources become available to implement In-Service. In the Dominican Republic, for example, a trained Teacher of the Deaf becomes a coordinator of mainstream education in the public schools where students with hearing loss are enrolled. She educates and informs teachers on hearing loss, the appropriate accommodations, and the unique learning needs of students with hearing loss.

Mainstreaming children with hearing loss in public schools is clearly difficult in many low- and limited- resource communities. And private schools are often inaccessible or unaffordable. Many schools do not accept children who cannot speak; however, fostering an understanding of hearing loss in schools can help reduce stigma and improve attitudes. Even a basic understanding can improve their response toward children coping with hearing loss.

Practitioners can refer to the PGV website for a complete guide to hearing loss awareness in schools entitled *Hearing Differences and Technology*. The program targets school age children and is available in English only. *Hearing Differences and Technology* invites parents (or practitioners) to implement 30- to 45-minute informational sessions. The handbook includes scripts, mini experiments, and child friendly materials on sound, hearing, and technology. The program contains 15 short segments that can be implemented in parts and given to children as young as three or four years of age. The goal is to build students' sensitivity and understanding of hearing, hearing assistive technologies, and communication needs of persons with hearing loss. You can find this program at www.greatervoice.com/learning modules.

# Comments on Community Collaboration

Even though low- and limited- resource communities may be challenged with early identification, treatment, family supports, and services to help children with hearing loss, collaboration among practitioners and organizations can affect development and expansion of services, programs and awareness of a cause. Alliances with non-government organizations and humanitarians can also facilitate outcomes when they share a common cause or similar mission. Clinics, schools, and social service agencies need to team up to strengthen outreach or improve views of disabilities in their communities. Together they can create awareness of childhood hearing loss and prevention, develop programs to support families, and reach persons with disabilities living at distances. Though clinics and practitioners are busy, relationships and effective communications need to be established to build capacity and expand supports given to families and persons with disabilities.

Being connected with other organizations and practitioners is essential because children with hearing loss may be suspected or diagnosed with additional conditions. At least 40% of children with hearing loss express other disabilities (Gallaudet Research Institute, 2008). Practitioners working with children place estimates at more than 50%. Appropriate diagnosis and services with trained professionals serving a particular area of special needs may be called for. Though rarely found in developing countries, specialists who come together in support of families with children with multiple special needs is clearly helpful. If children's language is significantly delayed due to a hearing loss, then it can compromise their cognition and learning. For this reason, collaboration and shared resources become that much more significant to tease out children's specific developmental, learning, and communication needs. When practitioners work together and engage in their communities, they share resources and knowledge to improve the outcomes of families and children they serve.

Although working collaboratively is challenging in low- and limited- resource communities, the diverse learning and communication needs of children and their parents might necessitate a team of specialists. In some situations, specialists may be able to travel to the homes of families to support, treat, and monitor children's progress. There are also families who are willing to travel for specialized therapy and other forms of direct services. In some communities, families are equally grateful when they can rely on multiple supports in one location. UMMEED Child Development Center in Mumbai, India is a great example of how collaborative teams support families of children with disabilities. The organization offers a range of services (developmental and educational assessments, occupational and speech therapies, and counseling), as well as many interdisciplinary programs (early intervention, autism, and school-based services). They often collaborate with organizations and people to offer specialized training and education courses. The organization also works with multiple schools to improve mainstream education for children with disabilities and their successes.

Further, non-government organizations and social service group interests might overlap on nutrition, maternal health, early childhood education, and other initiatives to benefit people and influence community understanding of the need at hand. When organizations with like-minded philosophies collaborate, they help in many ways: expand knowledge and skills, share human resources, bring together a network of people standing up for a cause, promote a need for services that might be lacking, help families attain health services. Lions International, Rotary, and other humanitarians participate in service missions to support and improve health, education, economic, and social services. Strong alliances and collaboration among charitable people create visibility of the needs in a community while simultaneously reducing the burden of human and financial resources on any one person or organization.

> Community engagement is "a dynamic relational process that facilitates communication, interaction, involvement, and exchange between an organization and a community for a range of social and organizational outcomes" (en.wikipedia.com).

## SUMMARY

According to the World Health Organization, 466 million people (nearly 6% of the world population) currently have some degree of disabling hearing loss, and estimates are expected to increase to over 900 million people by 2050 (WHO, March 2018). More than 3/4 of the world population of persons with hearing loss live in low- and middle- income countries. Though the number of children with hearing loss in many places is not conclusive (currently around 34 million), there are global efforts to advance diagnosis and prevent hearing loss.[89] The World Health Organization further states that 60% of hearing loss in these children can be prevented. Factors that induce hearing loss include noise pollution, disease, genetics, poverty, poor health, complications at childbirth, aging, and polluted waters.

What has been a joy to witness, however, is the growing interest and energy in hearing health and habilitation across the world over the last two decades. Programs are starting up and improving all the time. Clinics are becoming more equipped with audiometers, screening devices, tympanometry, and auditory brain stem monitors. Hearing assistive technologies are being dispensed at greater numbers than ever before, and cochlear implant programs have been established in many places around the world. Schools and ministries are implementing teacher training in early education and deaf education. Some hospitals and clinics are developing parent education courses that provide regularly scheduled workshops and hands-on learning experiences. And many communities are starting or strengthening parent support groups.

Even still, there is not enough support given to families coping with childhood hearing loss, particularly those families in remote or economically disadvantaged communities. Hearing health and education services for children and their families are greatly needed. Practitioners serving these populations intimately understand the challenges they face. They know how underprovided their services might be. They grapple with limited time and resources to care for hearing health needs effectively: resources for affordable hearing devices, technologies for proper diagnostics, trained professionals to counsel families, well-qualified technicians and Teachers of the Deaf.

Accompanying this is the explosion of electronic data. Information travels far more quickly today than it did ten or even five years ago. More and more practitioners are able to access resources on the internet and communicate with other service providers around the globe. Distance education programs and remote diagnosis are improving. Parents are also able to search the internet for information on communication methodology and technologies, and social media and online applications such as WhatsApp and Messenger are improving ways parents connect and become informed. More parents are learning about cochlear implants and digital devices; they are communicating with other parents about their experiences and concerns using the World Wide Web.

We know from informal assessments and analysis that training and education in hearing health, language development, and parenting skills are needed in low- and limited- resource communities. While certification and credentialing across clinical practices and social service agencies is often in demand, the hearing health and habilitation industry is working to build capacity and outreach to fulfill the need. Progress to address early childhood interventions and identification ensue. Vital to this development are parent focused interventions in psychological well-being that cannot be ignored.

As expressed throughout this resource, the supports caregivers receive must work from the inside out, coaching them on positive mindset, emotional awareness, character strengths, intrinsic resources, and leadership potential. Even as parents carry their grief and learn to cope, parents possess degrees of will, strength, and independence that can transform their mentality into empowered facilitators of their children's development (and parent support groups). Parents who draw upon their inner resources can learn to nurture their children in healthy and positive ways.

Parents' involvement is vital, and practitioners must find ways to foster parental well-being by informing and enabling parents in new ways. Coaching and empowering families of children with hearing loss must target domains of caregiver well-being expressed throughout this book. Parent groups and individualized parent consults become important opportunities. Parent supports must be present in everyday hearing health and habilitation practices throughout the world.

# PART FOUR

# SUPPLEMENTS:

**Comments on Disability**
**The Convention for Rights of Persons with Disabilities**
**Comments on Aural/Oral Communication**
**Listening and Spoken Language Therapy**
**How to Start A Parent Group**

# SUPPLEMENT I:

## COMMENTS ON DISABILITY

The word "disability" is a broad term defined several ways. The Oxford Dictionary states, "a disability is a physical or mental condition that limits a person's movements, senses, or activities." Merriam Webster further defines disability as "a physical, mental, cognitive, or developmental condition that impairs, interferes with, or limits a person's ability to engage in certain tasks or actions or participate in typical daily activities and interactions." In general, disability can describe any condition that limits or diminishes a person's ability to participate in life. Disability may be induced by brain injury, severe illness, hunger, or impaired mobility. Many people experience some form of disability at some point in their life; a broken arm or an ear infection are examples. These may be temporary but nonetheless are impairments that restrict mobility and hearing.

Disability should not define people but rather be the condition they experience. It calls to mind the need to understand differences and accept people with the unique challenges they may face.

Human response to disability varies and not everyone views disability in the same way. Although perceptions have evolved over decades, disability remains a complex topic and people are often excluded from participating in society because of their disabling condition. Barriers to their participation can be culturally, socially, environmentally, or economically induced.

Though data on persons with disabilities has been challenging to acquire in many countries, an estimated 15% live with disability in the world today. According to UNICEF, there are at least 93 million children with disabilities in the world. Low income populations are likely affected most, where it is less likely children attend school, access medical services, and participate in society. They are at risk of physical abuse and more vulnerable to illness and poor nutrition.

https://www.unicef.org/disabilities

Beliefs and perceptions of people with disability are sometimes imposed by culture, and attitudes toward persons with disabilities vary even within a community. These attitudes and potentially limiting beliefs might be passed from one generation to another. People may view disability through a small lens, especially if disabilities have never touched people's individual lives. It is not unusual to encounter places where disabilities are grouped into a single category. Ignorance about disability and disabling conditions may never have been properly addressed.

In the social view, people are disadvantaged not by their disabilities but by the limitations imposed on them. This not only means decreased access to education, health, employment, but also being excluded from participating in every day social activities most people take for granted (One Just World, 2009). Further, poorly designed roads and stairs impede travel for those using wheelchairs. The environment is compromised when neighborhoods and villages offer no access or accommodations for people with physical limitations (sight, hearing, mobility). Barriers also exist because of economics. Limited monetary resources prevent people with disabilities from accessing or purchasing appropriate technologies, private therapies, and medical treatment.[90]

People should not be defined by their disability or the barriers they face with disability. What is important to remember is that all persons regardless of a disability have abilities; the word "disability" contains the word "ability" so often missed. Language need not label or harm a person's identity; rather, it should describe a person's potential and their ability to fully engage and participate in society. There is a lot of pressure for people who are challenged by disabilities to "rise above," and they are asked to advocate for their needs and rights. Clearly, their successes contribute to reduced negativity about the barriers they face. Reducing stigma and discrimination requires an avoidance of negative connotations from everyone. In consideration of children with hearing loss, caregivers, therefore, must be equipped to transfer a self-empowered and positive mentality. Every person and every child with a disability expresses *ability*, and each has the right to fully participate in life, regardless of what humanity or culture might impose.

> Hearing loss is often referred to as an invisible disability, yet it affects all aspects of life: social, emotional, financial, political, physical. Children with hearing loss have *ability* and can learn, communicate, and thrive in life. These children depend on caregivers and practitioners to help them overcome barriers they may encounter. Opportunities to help them, therefore, must address children's unique learning and communication needs. Their success and inclusion in schools and communities is greatly enhanced when caregivers are empowered and engaged in social, emotional, and relational supports.

# The Convention for Rights of Persons with Disabilities (CRPD)

The CRPD responds to the urgent need for countries to embrace persons with disabilities and provides access to all for full participation and inclusion in society. Adopted by the United Nations in 2006, over 80% of member states ratified this human rights treaty by 2016.[91] Countries who ratified the agreement must develop policies to ensure rights are respectedand report back to the United Nations on their progress. It specifies, for example, "the need to change the perception of disability as vital to improving standard of life and inclusion for all with disability." It also recognizes that persons with disabilities are often not represented and should be included in policy creation. Further, CRPD promotes equal access to the rights specified in the treaty and ensures protection for women and children with disability.

The CRPD treaty promotes education and access to secondary and vocational training that reinforces the need for countries to provide inclusive education for persons with disabilities. This asks countries to implement policies and programs that not only include persons with disabilities in schools but also provide training initiatives that advance educational opportunities for persons with disabilities. For example, CRPD Article 23 states,

> "Children who have any kind of disability have the right to special care and support, as well as all the rights in the [CRPD], so that they can live full and independent lives." It goes on to declare, "children with disabilities shall have equal access, shall not be separated from their parents against their will, except when the authorities determine that this is in the best interest of the child, and in no case shall be separated from their parents on the basis of a disability."

CRPD protects and promotes inclusion and disability services, which drives attention to the caregivers who are the nuclei of support given to children. The full text on CRPD can be found on the United Nations website.[92]

Through the lens of the CRPD, the Sustainable Development Goals (SDGs) were established by the United Nations in 2015 to end poverty and hunger by 2030. Goals specify the need to improve maternal and child health, reduce poverty, and address major diseases such as HIV/AIDS and malaria. SDGs target member states of the United Nations and have 17 transformational objectives, one of which promotes quality education and another specifies well-being for all. Other goals strive to reduce inequalities by empowering and promoting social, economic, and political inclusion for all. Global indicators are being developed to measure the progress made in the implementation of the SDGs.

It is worth mentioning that there is a consensus to improve and strengthen data collection on both national and global levels for purposes of monitoring SDGs.[93] This should recognize the disability movement and invite the participation of persons with disabilities. And data on children with disabilities can be a vital force behind program need, development, and policy implementation that address inclusive education and well-being for these children, including those living in rural and impoverished communities.

Early childhood development experts across the world seek to protect young children with disabilities and at the same time promote their inclusion in all aspects of society. In general, practitioners working with families recognize the denial of young children with disabilities in schools and communities and want to improve their education and quality of life.

Factors that address child development include poverty, stigma/discrimination, parent/child interaction, violence/neglect, institutionalization, and economic distress. The United Nations report on early childhood education, which includes children with disabilities, asks stakeholders to find solutions to these barriers. Government policy, public health departments, and economic development initiatives can facilitate the advancement of children's rights and inclusion on a national or statewide scale.

Further, a World Report on Disability has been developed by the World Health Organization and the World Bank Group (2011). It is directed at policy-makers, practitioners, researchers, academics, development agencies, and civil society. This report aims to:

- provide governments and civil society with a comprehensive description of the importance of disability and an analysis of the responses provided, based on the best available scientific information.

- make recommendations for action at national and international levels."[94]

Accordingly, the inclusion of persons with hearing loss in society requires a broad reaching strategy that can build awareness and respect for their unique needs. Inclusion generally means a process of "bringing people together in shared physical settings where meaningful social interactions can be fostered and maintained" (Patterson, 2001).[95] Social inclusion, therefore, involves respect and empathy for people's abilities, regardless of disability or economic status.

Hearing loss as a disability is broad and multi-sectorial. Not all communication opportunities, early interventions, or educational options for children with hearing loss will align with a single government view, policy, or institutional focus. Policy and programs for children exist, but they may not be fully implemented nor developed to support the range of services children need or supports parents seek. It often requires parents become informed and rise-up to advocate for their children's needs and CRPD. Historically, parents who advocate for disability rights and their children's development have influenced progress and positive change in the system of supports for people with disabilities.

> The IDA Institute involves a consortium of hearing healthcare professionals from around the globe. They develop initiatives and share information in hearing rehabilitation that are focused on the needs and life situations of clients. Free tools, materials, and resources can be found on their website to help hearing care professionals deliver person centered care.
>
> www.idainstitute.org

# The Focus on Families

Over many decades of practice and theory, practitioners and policy makers have studied family and parent-centered practices and their effectiveness. The U.S Department of Health and Human Services created a policy statement on family engagement in 2016 that recognized the critical role of families from early childhood to elementary school age. Their goal is to identify core principles in family engagement, drive successful policy and program development, and recommend supports that successfully engage practitioners in family focused practices. The National Academies of Science, Engineering and Medicine released a report on Parenting Matters in 2016 to identify parenting knowledge, attitudes, and practices that support positive parent-child interactions. This document recognizes barriers and supports for parents' participation and recommends adoption of parent support strategies across government and nongovernment sectors. Though Parenting Matters is based on United States populations, it is a template for a global vision of services and support that caregivers and families need.[96]

> Every practitioner should begin with three important steps: support children with hearing loss, involve caregivers and family members, provide relevant and accurate information that applies to the learning and communication needs of children. Parenting journeys are challenging in low- and limited- resource communities, and the message is clear: parents play a critical role. Their participation and well-being are essentially the inroads to the successful futures for children with disabilities.

Across the world, practitioners seek to expand and improve patient focused or family centered supports that impact children's development and education in positive ways. Clinicians, university research fellows, non-government organizations, and scholars are doing amazing work to advance early childhood education, disability services, and parenting capacity and skills. There are dozens of resources to turn to for this, such as UNICEF, WHO, ECDAN, Early Childhood Development Action Group, Early Child Development Task Force, and the Academy of Science and Health. USAID, World Learning, and Partners for Every Child teamed up to craft a practical guide for frontline workers in low-and middle- income countries. The document targets family care across the spectrum of disability and is available for free (Family Care for Children with Disabilities, www.usaid.org, 2018).

# SUPPLEMENT II:

## COMMENTS ON AURAL/ORAL COMMUNICATION

Partners for A Greater Voice (PVG) was officially incorporated in 2001 to provide training and education in an aural/oral approach to communication (focused on auditory-verbal therapy) in developing countries and to serve both teachers and parents. The organization's first initiative began with an assessment in the Dominican Republic. With an interpreter, in just eight days, I toured five schools for the deaf, conferred with a dean at a university, conversed with the only official audiologist at the time, and met scores of teachers and parents. We encountered over one thousand children, most enrolled at schools for the deaf, and suspected there were far more children with hearing loss on this small Caribbean island.

On the last evening of the mission, we were on the north end of the island when I received a call from a woman living in San Andres, a town located in the south. She begged me to return to meet with dozens of parents that had gathered at her doorstep. I had spent the first two days in this town, meeting families and identifying thirteen children who had hearing loss. My interpreter, Estebania, was from this town. She had listened repetitively to my comments on hearing loss and auditory-verbal therapy all week long, and we decided to make the four-hour drive along a dark and dangerous highway to meet with these parents.

That evening, we stood under candle light without electricity facing dozens of parents, some we had not previously met, who had gathered with their children. None of these children were allowed to attend the public school, and most were not officially diagnosed; these parents knew their children had hearing loss and wanted help. Estebania took charge and explained all she had learned during our week together.

This was a turning point for me. I looked around at the group, handing crayons and paper to children, while Estebania engaged with a determination that I had not seen during any workshop or meeting we had together. Her voice was strong, her arms moved in all directions, and her eyes connected with everyone in the room. I looked at the parents, noticing their desperation for information and support to help their children. It was after 9 o'clock at night and parents were learning about hearing loss, hearing health, and communication opportunities for the first time.

My flight was early the next morning, but I knew I'd be back. There was an urgent cry for hearing health, aural/oral communication, and parent supports.

For the most part, people in developing countries do not know that children with hearing loss can learn to listen and develop intelligible speech. Sign language and manual forms of communication are more recognized options in the world, however, with appropriate use of Hearing Assistive Technologies (HAT) as well as auditory-based therapies, children can learn to communicate auditorily. Aural/oral communication is maximized when hearing loss is identified early in life, when children have access to HAT, when parents are informed and engaged with their children, and when auditory-based language-learning is provided by trained professionals. How well children develop oral fluency depends on many factors, including early diagnosis, anatomy of the ear and auditory nerve, functioning and appropriate technologies, listening skills development, and parent involvement.

Over ninety-five percent of profoundly deaf babies are born to hearing parents, the majority of whom want their children to talk, even when given information on communication opportunities. This decision may be linked to the familiarity of a hearing environment and perceptions of hearing loss. Stigma can be so harsh in developing countries that parents don't want their children to be different or perceived as having hearing problems. They want their children to speak and blend in with their communities. Even after telling parents about communication opportunities, the majority of families and teachers PGV has engaged with want auditory-verbal therapy and HAT for their children.

The opportunity to develop children's listening and conversational speech is maximized when identification and therapies begin before one or two years of age and when parents learn skills to help their children hear and speak. Professional guidelines recommend diagnosis by three months of age with hearing aid fitting and enrollment in therapy by six months of age. Guidelines for cochlear implantation is recommended by 12 months of age. Older children diagnosed with hearing loss can be prescribed HAT to explore how well these children respond to auditory stimulation (their hearing history is often unknown).

Spoken language is possible for children with mild, moderate, and even profound hearing losses when appropriate technologies and services in auditory-verbal therapy are available. Good hearing technology, such as digital hearing aids and cochlear implants, does not solve children's hearing loss but can facilitate access to hearing sounds and spoken language. In developing countries, support from experienced practitioners of auditory-based practices is desperately needed. Improving early diagnosis, advancing early interventions, increasing access to HAT, and professional training in aural/oral communication are often goals for practitioners. Parent focused training is also called for.

Collaborating with non-government organizations, humanitarians, and practitioners of auditory-based practices and speech and language can help boost training and initiate therapy programs focused on aural/oral communication. In 2001, PGV partnered with Sra. Onelia Aybar, director of education at a well-established school, Instituto de Ayuda al Sordo a Santa Rosa in Santo Domingo, Dominican Republic. Sra. Aybar focused on oral communication, yet her staff was starved for auditory-verbal education materials in Spanish, good functioning HAT for students, and supports to engage parents in their children's communication and learning. With qualified volunteer practitioners from the United States, PGV provided workshops and training to the school's teachers and hundreds of teachers from other parts of the country. Over ten intense years, PGV engaged in dozens of projects, including parent group initiatives that informed, supported, and empowered parents in new ways. Instituto de Ayuda al Sordo became the primary source of aural/oral communication information in the Dominican Republic, supporting hundreds of teachers throughout the country interested in aural/oral education.

## EXPANDING HEARING AND SPEECH SERVICES

Nearly every hearing health practice has the opportunity for practitioners to be forward thinking and strategic about advancing necessary services in support of children's aural/oral communication development. The best organizational model is when hearing aid and cochlear implant dispensaries, audiology clinics, counseling, parent support groups, and auditory-based therapies are offered in one location. This one-stop shop allows parents to learn the value and care of Hearing Assistive Technologies (HAT), to receive informational and emotional supports, and to identify and participate in practices that stimulate listening and spoken language. Organizations specializing in different services may need to collaborate.

Expanding these services in low- and limited- resource communities around the world are challenging yet are also emerging. For example, Dr. Elias Santa Hospital in Los Alcarrizos, Dominican Republic was founded by Centro Cristiano de Servicios Medicos (CCSM) as an ophthalmology hospital in 1984. In 2002, CCSM collaborated with a humanitarian audiologist from Australia working for Ears, Inc. to establish an audiology training program and audiology services under the direction of Donna Carkeet. A few years later, Partners for A Greater Voice collaborated with them to augment listening and speech therapy and parent supports, including the construction and establishment of an acoustically viable therapy room. Another example is AURED, which is located in Mumbai, India. This non-profit organization began in 1986 as a small center to support families and provide auditory-verbal therapy to children during the years when the auditory oral method was not well known in the country. AURED has supported hundreds of families and children with HAT from towns and cities throughout Maharashtra. They now have complete audiology, hearing, and speech services, as well as parent supports and counseling. They also provide professional development and training. AURED successfully maximizes listening and spoken language opportunities for children of all economic backgrounds.

As HAT expand across the globe, so too must aural/oral communication and family centered supports. Collaboration is essential to their success. Hearing clinics dispense and program hearing technologies and provide counsel to families. They can explore the feasibility of starting hearing and speech services and parent groups if not currently offered. Schools for the deaf can partner with audiology services and hospitals that support ear care in their countries and give clinics support. Building and equipping therapy rooms with help from service agencies or humanitarians may also be needed; local resources can be sourced for the construction.

Opportunities to solicit humanitarians or grants can also ignite speech and hearing services, parent education programs, therapy programs, and family centered services. The sustainability of aural/oral communication in low- and limited- resource environments may depend on such humanitarian and charitable support. Given the fact that clinics and schools in many of these communities are busy environments, greater human and financial resources are in demand. Grants, corporate discretionary funds, social service and non-government organizations, as well as humanitarian missions are increasingly available in today's world.

## **INVOLVING PARENTS**

Parents need to know how Hearing Assistive Technologies (HAT) work and how to maintain devices; they also need to understand how amplification and stimulation to the auditory cortex of the brain facilitates comprehension of a spoken language. In many cases, parents forget the importance of teaching children how to listen through audition when their children wear HAT. Helping children communicate auditorily must involve parents and intensive lessons to help these children learn to listen with the ears and not the eyes. Parents often rely on practitioners to do the job of teaching their children and need reminders that their children require practice listening and putting meaning to the sounds they hear. Helping children learn through the sense of hearing requires parents to gain aural/oral communication knowledge and skills. Parent workshops are great opportunities to demonstrate effective and practical ways to develop aural/oral communication; parents need to engage with their children.

What is amazing to see is when parents see the benefits of listening and spoken language in children with hearing loss. They respond with interest and enthusiasm, wanting to teach their children how to communicate orally. There are parents who develop a strong interest in aural/oral communication and make great progress with their children's oral development. These parents often share their successful experiences and step into a role that supports not only their children but also other families. Many parents become role models, and the success of their children demonstrates that children with hearing loss can learn to listen and talk.

In the Dominican Republic, for example, two parents with very low resource were trained by PGV and became parent specialists. They visited the homes of children with hearing loss, giving instructions on the use and care of HAT and offering tips to help parents communicate auditorily. They also encouraged parents to attend parent group meetings and to send their children to a school for the deaf they helped start. They became well regarded as specialists who understood aural/oral communication that was provided at the school. One parent facilitated learning to listen skills in young children who were given HAT for the first time.

Personalities are different, and parents face many choices as they learn grow and evolve as caregivers of children with hearing loss. Not all choose aural/oral communication for their children. HAT must be available and accessible. The hope is that all parents become empowered to help their children thrive, and that their journeys become happier ones as they learn to cope with hearing loss, manage their emotional, social, and informational needs, and help their children learn and communicate.

## DEVELOPING LISTENING SKILLS

Wearing Hearing Assistive Technologies (HAT) is only a first step in hearing and accessing spoken language. Children will not learn to talk with oral fluency unless parents and practitioners are involved in the process to develop their children's listening skills first. It is easy to take for granted every day sounds and language, but children who have hearing loss need to be taught the meaning of what they hear. While there are many audiologists who give HAT to children for self-esteem or safety in low- and limited- resource communities, developing listening skills begins with good auditory access.

Developing listening skills involves a continuum of detection, discrimination, identification, and comprehension of sounds and speech across hearing frequencies. This hierarchy in listening is fundamental to Aural-Oral Communication development. Children's sense of hearing develops as they make auditory connections and when they learn to put meaning to the sounds, words, and phrases they hear. Learning to listen is not equivalent to learning language. Think of learning to listen as a pathway to develop the auditory cortex of the brain. It is a skill development process that evolves differently for each child and is greatly influenced by appropriate services and parent participation.

Learning language is a complex process, and it is not solely based on wearing HAT. Spoken language requires acoustic accessibility of intelligible speech and a commitment to hearing in meaningful contexts. Auditory work/development involves cognitive building blocks. Hearing (listening) is the first-order event in developing spoken language and literacy. It requires practice and must embrace meaningful language and meaningful conversation (Carol Flexer, 2012).[97] Therapies and interventions help parents and their children engage in language learning and the process to help children maintain access to auditory information.

Children's progress in auditory-based practice is on-going, from birth and toddler years throughout school age. Auditory work must occur in children's natural environment. The younger children are when they experience sound awareness and auditory stimulation, the more likely they will experience outcomes in their ability to comprehend sounds, learn language, and engage in conversational speech. Children in low- and limited resource environment have successfully learned to talk with support from their parents and practitioners of aural/oral communication. PGV has seen remarkable progress in the field, especially as HAT gets dispensed more and more. However, families need to understand the importance of consistent amplification and their participation.

> "Every moment I have with my children, I imagine what might be going through their minds. I follow their eyes and movements, and I talk about everything that could be heard, seen, and touched. I squat down to their ear level and engage with them the intonation of my voice; I get close to them and describe what we are doing. The experiences we have together are a playground for learning and language development." ~ Joanne Travers

## LISTENING AND SPOKEN LANGUAGE THERAPY

Listening and Spoken Language (LSL) is based on auditory-verbal therapy and the process requires children with hearing loss to have access to Hearing Assistive Technologies (HAT). Regardless of the degree of hearing loss, when following an auditory-verbal approach, children can learn to process language. Children typically participate in therapy sessions with an Auditory-Verbal Therapist (AVT) or Listening and Spoken Language Therapist (LSLT), Some children receive additional therapy to meet their unique needs, while other children require fewer individual sessions. The number of sessions a child receives is not related to their age. Generally, individualized sessions given to children focus on development of their speech, language, and thinking skills through listening.

There are several domains of aural habilitation and hearing management that involve the dedication of parents and children as well as support from practitioners. These domains are expressed in a certification process and include ways to coach and guide families choosing an auditory verbal approach for their children. The methodology and certification of LSLS-Cert. AVT therapists follows ten principles requiring early diagnosis and intervention, state of the art amplification, caregiver coaching and guidance to facilitate listening and spoken language, and education alongside typically hearing peers. Visit www.agbellacademy.org for more information.

## Brief Comments on the Internet

There are also hundreds of resources online that practitioners and parents can turn to in this era of aural/oral communication. YouTube videos of therapy sessions, webinars, and industry related websites provide information on hearing technologies and ways to develop listening and spoken language. Material can be found by surfing the web and putting in key words: aural/oral, communication options, parenting children with hearing loss, auditory-verbal therapy, cochlear implants, hearing aids, assistive hearing technologies, hearing health, auditory-based practice, learning to listen with hearing technologies, etc. Prominent schools and organizations focusing on aural/oral communication can also be found by surfing the World Wide Web. There are organizations and individuals throughout the world that provide education and training in auditory-based practices and share their work. Some post recorded therapy sessions, articles, blogs, and PowerPoint presentations online. Many of these are available in different languages.

Information across the field of hearing and speech is available more than ever before. Material is even more accessible with translation technologies such as Google Translate, Speak & Translate, iTranslate, and TripLingo (for Androids). Many resources online are provided free and can be downloaded to personal computers, tablets, smart phones, and other mobile devices. Some universities and organizations may charge a subscription fee or charge for online courses.

# SUPPLEMENT III:

## How to Start a Parent Group

C*ollaboration* and *consistency* are the primary goals to keep in mind when stating a parent group. Perseverance, dedication, and a commitment to family engagement and parent education are also necessary. Finding people willing to invest time in the coordination and planning of informational and social gatherings is time consuming, but nonetheless important. Groups are invaluable opportunities for learning and empowering parents as well as their children. Addressing concerns about language learning, inclusion, stigma, and parenting are some reasons why parents must come together. Practitioners, parents, and children with hearing loss often benefit from a network of people coping with hearing loss in their communities.

Starting any parent group is a commitment; therefore, working collaboratively is important. Because environments and culture are different, it is prudent to explore parent group start-ups with practitioners and parents in your community. Before scheduling parent meetings, sit with others who share your interest and brain storm ideas to sustain the parent group. Ask parents of children you serve if a parent group is something they would like to help with. Find a dedicated practitioner or service provider to initially oversee the project. Working with a core group of people is an enormous asset to jump-start any parent group. The burden does not have to fall on one person; working as a team results in greater success.

Refer to the following suggestions:

- Set goals and establish objectives for the parent group you envision.
- Create a simple name that is culturally relevant and interesting.
- It's not necessary to legally incorporate a parent group unless you wish to do major fund raising or start an organization that can be listed as a corporation in your state or country. You might wish to keep things simple in the first year, and then determine if legalizing your organization is necessary.
- To incorporate a parent organization, you must consult local authorities regarding legal procedures.
- People may perceive an incorporated organization as more legitimate and professional.

- Organizations run by parents for parents are less threatening than government or political organizations and institutions.
- Establish a group of advisors and board members to oversee the direction of the business.
- Create a business plan and include financial and program expectations.
- Compile a list of parent names and contact information: address, cell phone number, child's name, child's date of birth. Gather relevant information such as degree of loss, cause of loss, school, and other useful data. (Create a file, using a computer, index cards, or paper folders.).
- If computers are accessible, create a database to manage contacts; update regularly.
- When you gather parents together, always create a list of attendees. Have parents sign in and update their information.

Initially meet with a small group of parents and practitioners who are committed to starting a parent group, even if this involves only three people. At this meeting, discuss purposes and goals. List the benefits most relevant to parents in your community. Answer questions such as, *how often can we hold these meetings, what information would parents be most interested in learning,* and *how might parents be able to help with these meetings*?

Finding a location that is convenient for parents is important. Parent group meetings should be held in places that can be accessed easily by transportation or by foot. Consider holding meetings at a well-known church, agency, or local school.

- A parent who works at an office building might have a meeting room parents can use on a weekend or evening.
- A local church or school may be willing to host a parent meeting at no cost.
- A parent may work in a company where there is a conference room or space to host groups of people.

Here are other considerations:

- Consider alternating between two locations in order to accommodate families.
- Consider a regional group meeting at a well-known location.
- Consider the number of families in any one town or region; seek out a parent who may be able to coordinate local meetings for families.

Set up regularly occurring or predictable meetings that can be easily remembered, such as the last Sunday or first Saturday of every month…be consistent. You may want to survey or ask parents what days and times work best. Evenings may work better for some while weekends may be better for families. You might decide to have parent-only meetings alternate with family gatherings.

For the first parent meeting, hold a general discussion about the benefits of parent-to-parent interaction and the strategic vision for the parent group. Allow parents to contribute to the conversation. Listen to parents and take notes about subject matter they have interest in.

- Take time to find out what parents want to learn and compile a list of topics.
- Create a formal or informal checklist of informational topics for parents. Let parents select three or four from the list.

Parent meetings should offer information that parents want to learn about (topic examples: nutrition, appropriate amplification, behavior management, establishing routines for the child at home, communication strategies, language development activities, disability laws, etc.). Select one theme for each meeting that is suggested by parents and determined a priority. Parent meetings must be educational and add value to the parent-to-parent experience.

- Plan out a program focus for the first three or four meetings.
- Build your program around the topic.
- Invite a teacher to present on a subject matter, such as literacy or the value of storytelling.
- Invite a pediatrician to talk about health and nutrition, such as vaccinations or good foods.
- Have an audiologist discuss troubleshooting or proper care of hearing assistive technologies.
- Find an experienced therapist or counselor to talk about child behavior, parenting, or socio-emotional growth of children.
- Use an exercise from this book, such as exploring parent emotions, assessing limiting beliefs, or coping strategies.
- Choose subject matter that helps parents reflect on their strengths and abilities to participate in their children's communication and learning.
- Share informational articles or a one-page summary of the topic you cover.
- Structure your meetings so they have a beginning, a middle, and an end. For example, begin with introductions, then present a topic, and end with time for parents to socialize over coffee/drinks/food.

Meetings come in all shapes and sizes, and they can be held at different venues. Meetings can be as simple as a gathering at a local park or at a home. Meetings also allow children to play and interact with each other.

- A parent meeting can offer food and drinks; some parents will bring such items.
- A parent meeting can be purely social and include the whole family: a sports event, a holiday celebration, a picnic, a dance performance.
- A parent who shows initiative can be invited to help coordinate a parent meeting, bring food, or promote the meeting via word of mouth.
- Limit meetings to two hours, or culturally appropriate length of time.
- Weekend gatherings or family events can extend to accommodate excursions.

Further:

- Always allow time for parents to meet and greet each other.
- Consider a social time in the middle of the program, in the event someone arrives late or must leave early.
- Consider play toys, books, or events for children to keep them occupied while parents engage in a learning experience.
- Every meeting must have an agenda. It should include some fun, and an opportunity for parents to socialize and enjoy meeting each other.

Always have a facilitator to keep the agenda on track and to navigate how parents can participate equally. Here are things to reflect upon:

- Encourage participation and ask people to be brief.
- Encourage equal amounts of sharing by all; avoid letting others dominate.
- Maintain positive outlook; discourage griping or complaining.
- Add humor and make parents laugh.

When planning events, always reach out to all parents to remind them and encourage their participation.

- Word of mouth and personal chats are the best invitations.
- Consider using a mobile phone application, such as WhatsApp or Facebook's Messenger.
- Hand out one-page flyers to families who walk into your office.
- Create a one or two-page annual or bi-annual newsletter that includes events, and circulate it to other clinics, schools, and health organizations working in your community.
- Post a flyer and calendar of events in the waiting room or reception area.
- If you have a website site, post a calendar of events on your front page.
- Display a large poster on the wall about your parent groups. Tape pictures from past events and include a few short sentences that highlight the benefits of your parent group meetings. Leave a blank space in the middle of the poster where you can write in the date, time, and location of an upcoming meeting, changing this each time a meeting is scheduled.

Parents like to be *invited* to parent group meetings, not told to attend. The main force behind parent groups is that people want to feel they belong, they can learn something, and that they develop meaningful friendships. Goals include bringing parents and families together, influencing parents' learning experience, and engaging families in their children's development.

*Words of advice:*

> Parent groups meetings are not personal counseling sessions. Find a qualified counselor or psychologist who can help parents in private.
>
> Stick to your agenda; don't allow conversation to move away from the topic you planned.
>
> Say, "That's a great topic. Would everyone like to discuss this at the next meeting?"

The suggestions in this supplement can be adapted to meet local interests and needs. Use as a guideline to start and organize parent groups, or to create a strategic plan to facilitate the success of your parent group projects. Practitioners are the best judge of their time, cultural environment, human resources, and skills needed to sustain parent support groups. Perhaps starting with a monthly and bi-annual meeting is initially called for; increase the number of times parents meet as more parents get involved. The more often parents meet, the more likely they are to become empowered, to improve their well-being, and to engage in positive journeys that help their children.

# SOURCES AND RESOURCES:

## ENDNOTES

[1] World Health Organization (WHO), "Hearing Loss and Deafness, Key Facts," (March 15, 2018). http://www.who.int/news-room/fact-sheets/detail/deafness-and-hearing-loss.

[2] WHO, "Childhood Hearing Loss, Act Now Hear's How," (2016). https://www.who.int/pbd/deafness/world-hearing-day/WHD2016_Brochure_EN_2.pdf.

[3] Grant initiatives, contact Joanne Travers, Executive Director of Partners for A Greater Voice at info@greatervoice.com.

[4] Joanne Travers, *About A Parent*, Oral Presentation at the 3rd annual Coalition for Global Hearing Health Conference, South Africa. 2012.

[5] Carol Ryff's Factors of Psychological Well-Being, "Happiness is everything, or is it? Explorations on the meaning of psychological well-being." *Journal of Personality and Social Psychology. Vol 57, No. 6,(1987): 1069-1081.*

[6] Martin E. P. Seligman, *Flourish: A Visionary New Understanding of Happiness and Well-being* (New York: Atria Paperback, 2013).

[7] Tal Ben-Shahar, Ph.D., "Overview Positive Psychology," Positive Psychology certification course, Whole Being Institute (Kripalu, May 2015).

[8] C. R. Snyder, Shane J. Lopwz, *The Handbook of Positive Psychology*, (New York: Oxford University Press, 2001).

[9] For a deeper understanding of positive psychology read *The Handbook of Positive Psychology* (C. R. Snyder, Shane J. Lopez, Oxford University Press: 2001).

[10] Tia Ghose, "Personality Type is Linked to Success and Happiness," *Live Science*, (Aug 23, 2013). Accessed January 20, 2019. https://www.livescience.com/39128-optimistic-realists-do-best.html.

[11] Karen Reivich and Andrew Shatte, *The Resilient Factor,* (New York: Three Rivers Press, 2002) 40.

[12] CL Green, JMT Walker, KV Hoover-Dempsey and HM Sandler, "Parents' Motivations for Involvement in Children's Education: an empirical test of a theoretical model of parental involvement." *Journal of Educational Psychology,* (2007) 532–544.

[13] Shenaar-Golan, "The Subjective Well-Being of Parents of Children with Developmental Disabilities: The Role of Hope as Predictor and Fosterer of Well-Being," *Journal of Social Work in Disability Rehabilitation* 15(2) (Apr-June 2016):77-95. doi: 10.1080/1536710X.2016.1162119.

[14] Manfred Hintermair, "Personal Resources, Parental Stress, and Social Emotional Growth of Deaf and Hard of Hearing Children," *The Journal of Deaf Studies and Deaf Education*, 11(4) (Oct. 2006): 493-513.

[15] Daniel J. Seigel, M.D. and Karen Hartzell, M.Ed., *Parenting from the Inside Out: How a Deeper Self Understanding Can Help You Raise Children Who Thrive*. (New York: Perigee Books, 2017).

[16] Tal Ben-Shahar, Ph.D., "Introduction to Positive Psychology." Positive Psychology Certification Course, Whole Being Institute, (Kripalu, May 1, 2016).

[17] Susan Folkman and Judith Moskowitz. *Positive Effect and the Other Side of Coping*. American Psychologist, 15(6) (2000): 647-54.
[18] Barbara Frederickson, *Positivity*, (New York: Three Rivers Press, 2009) 90-95.
[19] Pamela Schmidt, Psy., "Overview of Positive Psychology," a workshop at The Positive Psychology Summit, (Kripalu, June 3, 2017).
[20] Carol Dweck, *Mindset, the New Psychology for Success*, (New York: Ballantine Books, 2006).
[21] Shinrigaku Kenkyu, "Stress-buffering effects of benefit finding on the psychological stress' response in mothers of children with developmental disorders," *The Japanese Journal of Psychology* 85(4) (Oct. 2014):335-44.
[22] R.G. Tedeshi & L.G. Calhoun, *Posttraumatic Growth: Conceptual Foundation and Empirical Evidence*, (Philadelphia, PA: Lawrence Erlbaum Associates, 2004)
[23] C.G. Davis, S. Nolen-Hoeksema, & J. Larson, "Making Sense of Loss and Benefiting from the Experience." *Journal of Personality and Social Psychology* 75(2) (August 1998): 561-74.
[24] Geoffrey L. Cohen and David K. Sherman, "The Psychology of Change: Self-Affirmation and Social Psychological Intervention," *Annual Review of Psychology* (2014). http://psych.annualreviews.org
[25] Barbara Frederickson, *Positivity*, (New York: Three Rivers Press, 2009) 120-137.
[26] Daniel Siegel, MD and Mary Hartzell, M.Ed. *Parenting from the Inside Out: How a Deeper Self Understanding Can Help You Raise Children Who Thrive*, (New York: Penguin Random House: 2014) 232-233.
[27] Christina Gregory, PhD. "Understanding Stages of Grief, an Examination of Kubler-Ross Model," Psycom, Assessed February 13, 2019. https://www.psycom.net/depression.central.grief.html.
[28] Emily Holland, Certified Health Coach, "Side Affects of Worrying and What to Do About It," The Chopra Center, Blog accessed November 13, 2018. https://chopra.com/articles/the-side-effects-of-worrying-and-what-to-do-instead.
[29] en.wikipea.org
[30] C.W. Jackson et al, "Family Supports and Resources for Parents of Children who are Deaf and Hard of Hearing," *American Annals of the Deaf* 143 (2011) 343-362.
[31] Karen Mountney, "Parenting on a Low Income," *About Families* (March 2012). www.aboutfamilies.org.uk.
[32] LH Chaudron, PG Szilagyi, W Tang et al., "Accuracy of Depression Screening Tools for Identifying Postpartum Depression Among Urban Mothers," *Pediatrics*. 125(3) (2010). www.pediatrics.org/cgi/content/full/125/3/e609.
[33] DK Gjerdingen and BP Yawn, "Postpartum Depression Screening: Importance, Methods, Barriers, and Recommendations for Practice," *Journal of the American Board of Family Medicine* 20(3) (May 2007): 280–288.
[34] Morelli SA, Lee IA, Arnn ME, Zaki J., "Emotional and Instrumental Support Provision Interact to Predict Well-being." *Emotion*. 15(4) (2015): 484–493.
[35] Pamela Schmidt, M.Ed. LSW, "Human Happiness: Cultivating Resilience Through Resilience and Positive Psychology", presentation at the Positive Psychology Summit, (Kripalu, May 4, 2017).
[36] D. Goodley, C. Tregaskis, "Storying Disability and Impairment: Retrospective Accounts of Disabled Family Life," *Quality Health Research* (May 2006). https://doi.org/10.1177/1049732305285840.
[37] Russ Newman, "APA Resilience Initiative," *Professional Psychology: Research and Practice* 36(3) (June 2005): 227-229.
[38] Steven M. Southwick, MD, a recognized expert on the psychological and neurobiological effects of extreme psychological trauma, co-author of *Resilience: The Science of Mastering Life's Greatest Challenges* (Cambridge University Press, 2012).

[39] Bonnie Bernard, M.S.W., *Foundations of Resiliency Framework* (Technology, Health and Medicine: 2013).
[40] The Global Resiliency Report, "Resilience Enables Strategic Agility, How Resilience Delivers," *The Resilience Institute*, (2018). www.resiliencei.com
[41] Brady Hook, *A Guide to Resilience and Well-being*, The Resilience Institute. Accessed 2018. https://resiliencei.com/2018/07/guide-resilience-wellbeing/
[42] Maria Sorios, PsyD., "Resilience," presentation at Positive Psychology Summit, WholeBeing Institute, (Kripalu, May 1, 2017).
[43] Refer to Character Strengths in Part Two of *Coaching and Empowering Caregivers of Children with Hearing Loss, an approach to foster well-being.*
[44] Joseph Goldstein, *Mindfulness* (Sounds True, Boulder, CO, 2013).
[45] Empirical studies have offered ample evidence for the positive physiological and psychological effects of mindfulness for adults; immune function (Bartsch et al., 1992; Massion, Teas, Hebert, Wertheimer, & Kabat-Zinn, 1995), anxiety (e.g., Kabat-Zinn et al., 1992; Miller, Fletcher, & Kabat-Zinn, 1995); stress-level (e.g., Speca, Carlson, Goodey, & Angen, 2000).
[46] Lizabeth Roemer, Sarah Krill Williston, and Laura Grace Rollins, *Mindfulness and Emotion Regulation.* Accessed 2015. https://doi.org/10.1016/j.copsyc.2015.02.006
[47] Robert D. Seigel, *The Science of Mindfulness: A Research-Based Path to Well-being* (webinar: The Teaching Company, Harvard Medical School, 2014).
[48] M.G. Ramesh, B. Sathian, and E. Sinu, "The Efficacy of Rajayoga Meditation on Positive Thinking: An Index for Self-Satisfaction and Happiness in Life," *Journal of Clinical and Diagnostic Research* 7(10) (2013): 2265-2267.
[49] Eleonora Papaleontiou-Louca, *Metacognition and Theory of Mind* (Newcastle: Cambridge Scholars Publishing, 2008).
[50] Carol R. Ardous, "Creativity, Problem Solving and Innovative Science: Insights from History, Cognitive Psychology and Neuroscience," *International Education Journal 8(2)* (Nov 2007): 176-187.
[51] E. Anderson and G. Shivakumar, "Effects of exercise and physical activity on anxiety," *Psychiatry* (April, 2013).
[52] P. Lally, C.H.M. van Jaarsveld, W.H. Potts & J. Wardle, "How are Habits Formed: Modeling Habit Formation in the Real World", *European Journal of Social Psychology* 40(6) (2009): 998-1009.
[53] Margaret Wehrenberg, PsyD, *Depression Management Techniques, How your Brain Makes You Depressed and What You Can Do to Change It,* (Norton W.W. & Company Inc: 2011).
[54] Beverly Engel L.M.F.T., "Using the Practice of Self-Kindness to Cope with Stress Self-Kindness: An Important Aspect of Self-Compassion," *The Compassion Chronicles, Psychology Today,* blog posted on June 19, 2018.
[55] "Different Learning Styles." Scholastic Parents (Nov. 6, 2012). Accessed December, 2018. https://www.scholastic.com/parents/family-life/creativity-and-critical-thinking/learning-skills-for-kids/different-learning-styles.html.
[56] L.R. Diaconu-Gherasim, C. M irean, "Perception of Parenting Styles and Academic Achievement: The Mediating Role of Goal Orientations." *Learning and Individual Differences*, 49 (2016): 378-385.
[57] D.G. Myers, *Psychology: Eighth Edition in Modules.* (New York: Worth Publishers; 2010).
[58] Daniel J. Siegel, M.D. and Karen Hartzell, M.Ed. *Parenting from the Inside Out: How a Deeper Self-understanding Can Help You Raise Children Who Thrive* (New York: Perigee Books, 2017)
[59] Daniel J. Seigel and Karen Hartzell, *Parenting from the Inside Out.*
[60] K. M. Sheldon and S. Lyubomirsky, "How To Increase and Sustain Positive Emotion: The Effects of Expressing Gratitude and Visualizing Best Possible Selves." *Journal of Positive Psychology 1(2)* (2006): 73-82.

⁶¹ Adapted from Megan McDonough's "Best-Self Exercise," presented at The Positive Psychology certification course, WholeBeing Institute, (Kripalu, May 2, 2015).

⁶² J.B. Avey, R.J. Reichard, F. Luthans, K.H. Mhatre, "Meta-analysis of the Impact of Positive Psychological Capital on Employee Attitudes, Behaviors, and Performance," *Human Resource Development* Q 22(2) (2011): 127–152.

⁶³ Manfred Hintermair, "Parental Resources, Parental Stress, and Socioemotional Development of Deaf and Hard of Hearing Children." *The Journal of Deaf Studies and Deaf Education* 11(4) (October 2006): 1. https://doi.org/10.1093/deafed/

⁶⁴ Karen West, Elliott Stixrud, and Brian Reger, "Assessment: What's Your Leadership Style?" *Harvard Business Review* (June, 2015).

⁶⁵ Karen Reivich, Ph.D. and Andrew Shatte Ph.D., *The Resilience Factor* (New York: Three Rivers Press, 2002) 262.

⁶⁶ Virginia Maglio, MS and Joanne Travers, MIM, "Leadership and Trust," (Partners for A Greater Voice: 2017). www.greatervoice.com/articles.

⁶⁷ Larina Kase, PsyD, MBA, "Great Leaders are Greater Decision-Makers, Qualities to Take the Paralysis out of Decision Making," *Pepperdine Graziadio Business Review* 13(4) (2010).

⁶⁸ Daniel Goleman, *Emotional Intelligence* (New York: Bantam Books, 2005) 42-45.

⁶⁹ Peter Salavoy and John D. Mayer, *Emotional Intelligence* (New York: Baywood Publishing Company: 1990).

⁷⁰ Sumathy.L and Madhavi.C, "Influence of Emotional Intelligence on Decision Making by Leaders," *American International Journal of Social Science* 4(1) (February, 2015): 134.

⁷¹ Roger R. Pearman, *Introduction to Type and Emotional Intelligence: Pathways to Performance* (CA: CPP Mountain View, 2002) 11.

⁷² Kimberly J Saudino, PhD, "Behavioral Genetics and Child Temperament," *Journal of Developmental and Behavioral Pediatrics* 26(3) (June, 2005): 214-223.

⁷³ Christopher Peterson & Martin E.P. Seligman, *VIA Classification of Character Strengths and Virtues, A Handbook and Classification* (Oxford: Oxford University Press, 2004).

⁷⁴ Ryan M. Niemiec, PsyD., *Character Strengths Intervention, A Field Guide for Practitioners* (Boston: Hogrefe, 2017).

⁷⁵ Ryan M. Niemiec, PsyD., *Mindfulness and Character Strengths, A Practical Guide to Flourishing* (Boston: Hofrefe, 2014) 37-41.

⁷⁶ Ryan M. Niemiec, PsyD., "Learning to Unleash What's Best in You and Your Clients," *Character Strengths Intervention Master Class;* webinar (November 20, 2018).

⁷⁷ R. M. Ryan and E. L. Deci, (Eds.), "Self-determination Theory and The Facilitation of Intrinsic Motivation, Social Development, and Well-being," *American Psychologist* 55 (2002) 68-78.

⁷⁸ David Luterman, D.Ed., *Counseling Parents of Hearing-Impaired Children*, (New York: Little Brown Company, 1979) 26.

⁷⁹ Daniel J. Seigel and Karen Hartzell, *Parenting from the Inside Out* (NY: Perigee Books, 2017) 98.

⁸⁰ Jason Hangauer, Ph.D., NCSP Emily Shaffer-Hudkins, Ph.D., NCSP, "Engaging Caregivers to Follow-Through with Intervention Strategies," presentation at Bay Area Early Steps, September 23, 2013. Accessed January, 2019. http://www.independentlivinginc.com/wordpress/wp-content/uploads/2010/12/September-27-2013-Coaching-Cargivers-Final-PDF-Version-to-Publish.pdf

⁸¹ Carla Peterson et al. "Enhancing Parent–Child Interactions Through Home Visiting: Promising Practice or Unfulfilled Promise?" *Journal of Early Intervention*, 29(2) (2007): 134.

⁸² Dathan Rush, PhD. CCC-SLP, "From Couching to Coaching: How do we get families engaged in early intervention?" *The ASHA Leader Vol. 23* (October, 2018): 46-52.

[83] David Luterman, *Counseling Parents of Hearing-Impaired Children.*
[84] "Best Practices in Patient-Centered Care", Conference Proceedings; Sept. 26-27, 2013; Armstrong Institute; Johns Hopkins University, Baltimore, Maryland. www.hopkinsmedicine.org/armstrong/patient-centered-care-study.
[85] What Is Locus of Control? "A to Z of Brain, Mind, and Learning." Accessed Dec. 2018. www.learninginfo.org/locus-of-control.htm
[86] Ed Diener, "Bringing the Science of Happiness to Life." *Pursuit of Happiness* (2018).
[87] Rebecca Henderson, Andrew Johnson, Sheila Moodie, "Parent to Parent Support for Parents with Children Who are Deaf or Hard of Hearing: A Conceptual Framework." *American Journal of Audiology* 1–12 (Dec. 2013).
[88] Gerri Mattson and Dennis Z. Kuo, "Psychosocial Factors in Children and Youth with Special Health Care Needs and Their Families," Committee on Psychosocial Aspects of Child and Family Health, Council on Children with Disabilities, *Pediatrics* 143 (January, 2019): 1. Accessed Jan. 2019 AAP Gateway. http://pediatrics.aappublications.org/content/pediatrics/143/1/e20183171.full.pdf
[89] WHO, "Deafness and Hearing Loss" (March 2019). Accessed March 2019. https://www.who.int/news-room/fact-sheets/detail/deafness-and-hearing-loss
[90] Charlotte McClain Nhlapo, "Focus on People with Disabilities, Action for the World's Poor and Hungry People," Beijing (World Bank: Oct 18, 2007). Accessed January, 2019. https://www.slideserve.com/raja-pena/focus-on-people-with-disabilities.
[91] "Disability, Rights, and Sustainable Development," *Global Disability Rights Now.* (Christ Blind Mission (CBM)). Accessed January 2019. https://www.globaldisabilityrightsnow.org/infographics/link-between-sustainable-development-goals-and-crpd.
[92] United Nations - Disability, Department of Economic and Social Affairs, "Convention on Rights of Persons with Disability (CRPD)." Accessed October, 2018. https://www.un.org/development/desa/disabilities/convention-on-the-rights-of-persons-with-disabilities.html.
[93] International Disability Alliance, "Disability Data Advocacy Working Group." Accessed Dec. 2018. www.internationaldisabilityalliance.org/content/indicators-sustainable-development-goals.
[94] World Health Organization and The World Bank, *World Report on Disability*, (WHO and World Bank: 2011). Accessed Dec. 2018. https://www.who.int/disabilities/world_report/2011/en/
[95] I. Patterson, "Serious Leisure as a Positive Contributor to Social Inclusion for People with Intellectual Disabilities." *World Leisure Journal* 43(3) (2001): 16-24.
[96] Vivian L. Gadsden, Morgan Ford, and Heather Breiner, Editors, *Parenting Matters, Supporting Parents of Children 0-8*, (National Academies of Sciences, Engineering, and Medicine: 2016). http://www.nap.edu/21868
[97] Carol Flexer, Ph.D., CCC-A; LSLS Cert. AVT, "Auditory Brain Development: The Key to Listening, Language, and Literacy," March, 2012. Accessed Jan 2019. www.carolflexer.com.

# BOOKS

## RELATED TO POSITIVE PSYCHOLOGY:

*Authentic Happiness: Using the New Positive Psychology to Realize Your Potential* by Dr. Martin Seligman. (New York: Atria Books, first published in 2002).

*Authentic Strengths* by Fatima Doman. (Nevada: Next Century Publishing, 2006).

*Between Parent and Child* by Dr. Haim G. Ginott (1965); reprint by Dr. Alice Ginott and Dr. H. Wallace Goddard. (New York: Three Rivers Press, 2003).

*Buddha's Brain, the practical neuroscience of happiness, love and wisdom* by Rick Hanson. (California: New Harbinger Publications, 2009).

*Character Strengths and Virtues, A Handbook and Classification* by Christopher Peterson and Martin E.P. Seligman. (Oxford: Oxford University Press, 2004).

*Emotional Intelligence* by Daniel Goleman. (New York: Bantam Books, 2005).

*Flourish, A Visionary New Understanding of Happiness and Well-being* by Dr. Martin E. P. Seligman. (North Sydney, N.S.W. Australia: William Heinemann, 2012).

*Flow and the Foundations of Positive Psychology* by Dr. Mihaly Csikszentmihalyi. (Dordrecht: Springer, 2016).

*Happier* by Tal Ben-Shahar, Ph.D. (New York: McGraw-Hill, 2007).

*Learned Optimism: How to Change Your Mind and Your Life* by Dr. Martin Seligman. (London: Nicholas Brealey Publishing, 2018).

*Mindfulness and Character Strengths: a Practical Guide to Flourishing* by Dr. Ryan M. Niemiec. (Toronto: Hogrefe, 2014).

*Mindset, the New Psychology of Success* by Carol Dweck, Ph.D. (New York: Ballantine Books, 2016).

*Mindset:Changing the Way You Think to Fulfill Your Potential* by Dr. Carol Dweck. (London: Robinson, 2017).

*Parenting from the Inside Out: How a Deeper Self-understanding Can Help You Raise Children Who Thrive* by Daniel J. Seigel, M.D. and Karen Hartzell, M.Ed. (New York: Perigee Books, 2017).

*Positivity* by Dr. Barbara L. Fredrickson. (New York: Three Rivers Press, 2009).

*The Brain that Changes Itself, Stories of Personal Triumph from the Frontiers of Brain Science* by Norman Doidge, M.D. (New York: Penguin Books Limited, 2007).

*The Handbook of Emotional Intelligence: The Theory and Practice of Development, Evaluation, Education, and Application—At Home, School, and in the Workplace*, Reuven-Bar-On and James D.A. Parker, Editors. (San Francisco, CA: Jossey-Bass, 2000).

*The Instinct to Heal* by David Servan-Schreiber, MD, PhD. (U.S.A.: Rodale Inc., distributed by Holtzbrinck Publishers, 2004).

*The Resilient Factor: 7 Keys to Finding Your Inner Strength and Overcoming Life's Hurdles* by Karen Reivich, Ph.D. and Andrew Shatte, Ph.D. (New York: Broadway Books, 2003).

# OTHER BOOKS

## RELATED TO HEARING HEATH AND HABILITATION:

*Audiology in Developing Countries* edited by Bradley McPherson and Ron Brouillette. (New York: Nova Science Publishers, 2008).

*Auditory-Verbal Practice, Family-Centered Early Intervention* by Ellen A. Rhoades, Ed.S., LSL CERT.AVT and Jill Duncan, Ph.D. LSL CERT AVT. (U.S.A: Charles C. Thomas Publisher Ltd., 2017).

*Auditory-Verbal Therapy: For Young Children with Hearing Loss and Their Families, and the Practitioners Who Guide Them.* Estabrooks, W., Macliver-Lux, K., and Rhoades, E.A. (San Diego, CA: Plural Publishing, 2016).

*Children with Hearing Loss, Developing Listening and Talking* by Elizabeth B. Cole and Carole Flexor. (San Diego, CA: Plural Publishing, 2011).

*Developmental Profiles, Pre-birth Through Twelve,* by K. Eileen Allen and Lynn R. Marotz. (Canada: Wadsworth Cengage Learning, 2007).

*Helping Children Who Are Deaf* by Sandy Niemann, Devorah Greenstein, and Darlena David. (U.S.A: The Hesperian Foundation, Early Assistance Series for Children with Disabilities, 2004).

*Parents and Teachers: Partners in Language Development* by Audrey Ann Simmons-Martin, Ed.D. and Karen Glover Rossi, M.A. (U.S.A: Alexander Graham Bell Association, 1990).

## POSITIVE PSYCHOLOGY WEBSITES:

Positive Psychology Center - http://www.ppc.sas.upenn.edu

Dr. Barbara Fredrickson, Finding Happiness - http://www.positivityresonance.com

VIA Institute - http://www.viacharacter.org

Dr. Ryan Niemiec - http://www.ryanniemiec.com

WholeBeing Institute - https://wholebeinginstitute.com

## HOW TO CONTACT
### Partners for A Greater Voice:

Joanne Travers, info@greatervoice.com
Post Office Box 734, Ipswich, Massachusetts 01938, U.S.A.
1.978.312.1200 cellular (U.S.A.) / www.greatervoice.com

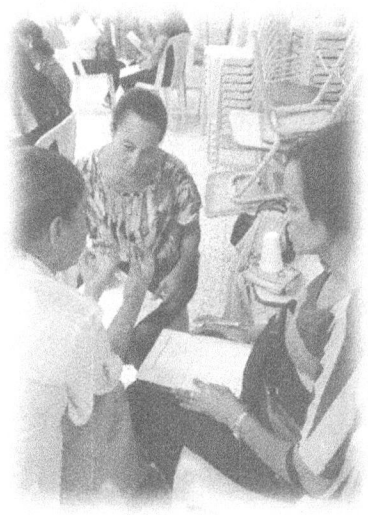

# Acknowledgements

My journey to fully recognize and understand caregiver well-being evolved over twenty years of parenting two children with disabilities, coordinating over thirty-five international training and education missions for the non-profit Partners for A Greater Voice, Inc. (PGV), as well as listening to hundreds of stories from parents of children with hearing loss. I appreciate and warmly regard the experiences I have had with parents, practitioners of audiology, and educators of the deaf and hard of hearing. Inspired by their passion to see children with hearing loss reach their full potential in mainstream society, I gained such valuable perspective from these personal and professional relationships.

I am grateful to have worked with over a thousand parents from around the world who taught me about the challenges they face with limited services or non-existing supports in education and hearing health. The struggles these caregivers endured and managed were lessons in resilience, empathy, motivation, leadership, and the power of positivity. I had the brilliant experience of living through the eyes and hearts of caregivers in developing countries who learned to cope with hearing loss and who desired mainstreamed experiences for their children. More than I ever hoped for, I discovered what I believed to be a crucial path to a healthy and happy parenting journey.

More than seventy volunteer partners engaged in dozens of PGV international missions to the Dominican Republic, India, and Honduras, each person bringing individual strengths and skills to our training. Hearing health and aural/oral communication is vastly rich with information and perspective, and knowledge from a diversity of people enhanced the skills of practitioners we worked with as well as my own understanding of early interventions, mainstream education, inclusion, literacy development, socio-emotional growth of a child, and caregiver supports.

I want to thank all educators who volunteered on PGV training missions to coach and guide Teachers of the Deaf in other countries and would like to mention a few of them here: Laura Peterson, Marianne Watson, Jane Driscoll, Olga Corral, Vahishtai Daboo, Barbara Manning, Lyndsay Rodriguez, Michael Moon, Carla Sanchez, Diana Sanchez, Christine Derosier, Amanda Esar, Katelyn Driscoll, Uma Gokhale-Soman. As practitioners of auditory-based practices, they embraced PGV's international vision that aural/oral education is possible for children in low resource communities. I am grateful for their partnership, their mission preparation, and their direct and indirect support given to me and the families and schools we served. From the goodness of their hearts, they enrich the lives of children with hearing loss and fill the world with greater understanding of family interventionism, language and literacy development, and the meaning of collaboration. Because of their efforts, aural/oral communication is making its way into low resource communities.

I am also grateful for doctors of audiology who supported our missions and dispensed hearing technologies to children: Marissa Mendrygal Williams, Todd Sauter, Dierdre Remick-Anderson, Lisa Walker, Marilyn Neault, Miguel Evangelista, Genesis Troncoso, and Misael Restituyo. My understanding of hearing health is greatly improved because of their honorable volunteerism and knowledge in pediatric audiology. Hundreds of children with hearing loss access good hearing because of their service. Hearing Assistive Technologies (HAT) have advanced in recent decades, and as hearing services and health practices continue to evolve in the developing world, my hope is that all audiologists put parents' psychological well-being first.

So many others influenced the PGV journey and mission success: Estebania Concepcion, Onelia Aybar, Grace Alice Guerrero, Carol Serna, Neil Reimer, Iraida Williams, Vahishtai Daboo, Yadixa Messina, Casilda Jeminez, Diorka Nolasco, Alison Miniter, Kelly Deroche, Frank Lepine, Gayla Guignard, Fatema Jagmag, and John Anderson. They provided me with a deep appreciation for the complex and diverse needs of children with hearing loss, parent education and supports, mainstream education, and inclusion of children with hearing loss.

I also thank audiologist Dr. Richard Seewald and psychologists Amy Szarkowski and Donna Mayerson. I warmly regard their personal interest in the well-being and empowerment of caregivers who cope with childhood hearing loss. They provided meaningful critique about the book's content and usability. Support from all three professionals helped me develop and home in on essential topics. I am forever grateful for their kindness and belief in me.

I gratefully acknowledge my board of directors Richard Denton, Virginia Maglio, and Dr. Brian Alper for their unconditional support and encouragement to get this book into print. Past Directors Laura Peterson, Neil Reimer, Jane Driscoll, Barbara Manning, Christyne Vachon, and Mark Batitte augmented PGV's training and mission focus, which is now contained in this book. I am ever thankful and appreciative of their involvement in PGV.

I would also like to acknowledge people who reviewed this book: Onelia Aybar, Director of Education, Instituto de Ayuda al Sordo Santa Rose, Dominican Republic; Nicole Hunter, Senior Administrator, Elias Santana Hospital, Dominican Republic; Fatema Jagmag, Audiologist, Maharashtra, India; Vahishtai Daboo, LSLT, Mumbai, India; Ron Bruillette, PhD, SLP; Megan McDonough, Executive Officer, Whole Being Institute, U.S.A.; Dr. James Saunders, Coalition for

Global Hearing Health; Dr. Richard Seewald, Canada; Dr. Ola Bolusanya, Nigeria. Their appreciative comments are a telling argument for this book as an important resource for practitioners and parents.

Professional editing and copy editing was provided by Stephen Kuntz, a professor of English working in Alberta, Canada. I enjoyed working with him and appreciate his coaching and writing expertise to help me finish this book. I extend a hug to my friends Suzanne Hodson, Early Childhood Practitioner, and Nancy Williams for proofreading the book.

I am blessed with a financial contribution from Hear The World Foundation (HTW) to support PGV's training and empowerment approach in book form. HTW's global assistance is given to humanitarians and service driven organizations that improve the quality of life and environment for people who cope with hearing loss. Coordinators Louise Sen's and Elena Toressani's faith and confidence in my experience and insight is greatly appreciated. Because of HTW support, PGV can donate a hard copy of this book to one hundred practitioners in low- and limited- resource communities at no charge.

Above all, I am grateful for my children, Tori and Matthew, and my devoted husband Paul. I can never say thank you enough for their trust in me and love. They taught me patience, perseverance, strength, sacrifice, and determination. I am forever grateful for 25 years of love, encouragement, and support blessed upon me by my husband. This book would never exist without my cherished family and their faith in me.

## About the Author:

Joanne Travers is a consultant, parent advocate, and motivational coach engaged in supporting and educating caregivers of children with hearing loss and practitioners who serve them. Her experience as a parent, raising two children with hearing loss, influenced her decision to commit to the hearing health and habilitation industry after twelve years of business and management experience in international economic development, telecommunications, and media production. Joanne founded Partners for A Greater Voice in 2001 and has completed over 36 international training and education missions to the Dominican Republic, Honduras, and India with support from more than 65 volunteer practitioners and parent specialists.

Her journey and advocacy efforts began when her two children were born with hearing loss and other disabilities in the mid 1990's. She supported their hearing and learning needs in mainstreamed schools while helping other families. Inspired by her children, she established Parent Connection in 1995. This parent group was created to support families who chose listening and spoken language in her home state. Joanne spearheaded this network for over a decade. Its success led to incorporating a state chapter of Alexander Graham Bell Association (A.G. Bell), currently sustained by the collaborative efforts of parents. In 1997, Joanne wrote a handbook called *Hearing Differences and Technology,* and for more than ten years she implemented this awareness program in public schools to break the stigma of hearing loss.

Involved in many social service organizations and advocacy initiatives, Joanne was elected twice to serve as a Director of A.G. Bell (6 years), and she served as a director on the board of the Coalition for Global Hearing Health (6 years). She is a Parent Advocate, trained by the Federation for Children with Special Needs in Massachusetts. She was a facilitator of the Parent Advocacy Training (PAT) project that was developed by A.G. Bell Association. Joanne was an Advisor to the Commissioner of the Deaf and Hard of Hearing in the state of Massachusetts. She was hired as an interim child specialist for the Department of Case Management and Social Services at the Massachusetts Commission for the Deaf and Hard of Hearing. Joanne also served as president and international coordinator of her local Rotary Club and served as district chair of international vocational programs. Joanne holds a Masters in International Management (MIM) and has a bachelor's degree in business, communications, design. She has a Certificate in Positive Psychology. Joanne is also a yoga teacher with over 650 hours of professional training and 1000 hours of teaching experience.

*Coaching and Empowering Caregivers of Children with Hearing Loss, an approach to foster well-being* is a culmination of Joanne's diverse and passionate experience.

www.ingramcontent.com/pod-product-compliance
Lightning Source LLC
Chambersburg PA
CBHW080434230426
43662CB00015B/2269